365
INSPIRATIONAL
QUOTES

365

INSPIRATIONAL

Quotes

a year of daily wisdom
from **GREAT THINKERS,**
BOOKS, HUMORISTS and more

ALTHEA
PRESS

CONTENTS

FOREWORD

FOR MUCH OF MY LIFE, especially in my work as a motivational speaker, coach, and author over the past 15 years, I've been a bit obsessed with quotes. I display them throughout my house, include them on calendars, and regularly post them on social media. For me, it doesn't matter where the quote comes from—an author, artist, politician, comedian, movie, book, teacher, scholar, or even a friend or family member. If it resonates with me, I'll take it . . . and I'll probably want to share it with you.

In the pages that follow, you'll be inspired by a unique and diverse list of quotes—from people like Vincent van Gogh, Tina Fey, Babe Ruth, and Elon Musk and from sources like the Quran, the Bible, and *Winnie-the-Pooh*. The truth is, we can find wisdom and inspiration from many different people and places; we just need to be looking for it.

From my experience working as a coach for many years, I understand the power of daily practices. From meditation and exercise to journal writing and much more, my own daily practices are essential to my life and well-being. And, in working with people from all walks of life, I've seen how transformational simple daily practices can be. This book is meant to be part of your daily practice; you can allow the power of each quote to impact how you start or end your day, and what you focus on.

Inspiration is vital to just about every aspect of our lives, yet it can be elusive. With more technology and devices in our lives than ever before, it's easy to get distracted, to remain insatiably busy, and to lose touch with our inspiration. If we aren't mindful, we can get caught up in the drama, negativity, and hyper pace of the world in which we live. These simple, but powerful, quotes can help open your mind and heart and remind you what truly matters in life, which is no small thing.

When I was writing my first book a number of years ago, I would often get stuck—my fears, doubts, and insecurities would take over and make it difficult for me to move forward. I found a few healthy (and many unhealthy) ways to deal with my bouts of writer's block (a.k.a. lack of inspiration), which at times was just plain old procrastination (a.k.a. fear).

One of the most productive techniques I found to deal with these issues was to search the Internet for inspirational quotes. Sometimes I was able to take the quotes I found and use them in my book; other times, they would help me expand my mind, think about something in a different way, or even just laugh. One weekend in the summer of 2006, as I was struggling to finish a chapter of that first book, I came across a quote I had not seen before, but that made me laugh out loud:

> *"Be yourself; everyone else is already taken."*
> *—Oscar Wilde*

This poignant quote resonated with me at the time because it made me realize I was *trying* to do what I thought I was *supposed* to do—write a "good book"—instead of actually writing from my heart and sharing my own unique perspective. It left such a strong impression that I included it inside that first book, and used it as the title of my second book, which came out just a few years later.

Enjoy this book! Allow its wisdom, wit, and inspiration to sink in . . . and soak them up as much as you can. In a world where it's easy to find cynicism, resignation, negativity, and constant complaining, it sometimes takes a radical act of courage and self-care to focus on inspiration and what truly matters.

Mike Robbins

Novato, California
October 2015

A NOTE FROM THE EDITOR

INSPIRATION IS ALL AROUND US . . . but it's nice to have some of its gems contained in one place. Within these pages, you'll find a powerful collection of quotes from great minds, like Albert Einstein and Oscar Wilde, as well as from some classic books, films, speeches, and more. We've all known the experience of reading an unforgettable book or hearing an inspiring interview, or savored the lyrics to a moving song that seemed to be speaking directly to us, to be made just for us right then, in that moment. These happy coincidences allow us to understand that, while life's journey seems sometimes solitary, there are others who have walked the same path and even stumbled in the same places along the way—including the best and brightest.

This diverse collection of quotes will infuse your day with appreciation, encouragement, and wisdom. Take this book with you as you start or end your day, or whenever you need an uplifting pick-me-up. Although the quotes are aligned to days of the year, there's no right or wrong way to read it. Dive in from the beginning, read it backward, or pick a page at random—no matter your method, you'll receive the same nuggets of inspiration covering a wide range of themes, from embracing creativity to achieving gratitude to falling in love.

Where appropriate, you'll find quotes tailored to all of the major U.S. holidays, and even some of the little ones too (like April Fool's Day and Groundhog Day) as well as some international religious holidays.

No matter your circumstances, whether you're enduring a prolonged rough patch or simply seeking some moments of quiet inspiration to temper your busy schedule, there is something here for you—365 days of the year.

1

THIS IS WHERE IT ALL BEGINS. EVERYTHING STARTS HERE, TODAY.

DAVID NICHOLLS, AUTHOR

Even when the world throws its worst and then turns its back, there is still always hope.

PITTACUS LORE, AUTHOR

If life is a bowl of cherries, what's inside of it?

—

JOSH STERN, AUTHOR

4

JANUARY

WE HAVE WITHIN US AN EXTRAORDINARY CAPACITY FOR LOVE, JOY, AND UNSHAKABLE FREEDOM.

JACK KORNFIELD, AUTHOR

5

JANUARY

The reason birds can
fly and we can't is
simply because they
have perfect faith,
for to have faith
is to have wings.

———

J. M. BARRIE, AUTHOR

6

JANUARY

Sadness is more or less
like a head cold—with
patience, it passes.

———

BARBARA KINGSOLVER, AUTHOR

WHAT GOOD IS WARMTH WITHOUT COLD TO GIVE IT SWEETNESS?

JOHN STEINBECK, AUTHOR

*May you be filled
with loving kindness.
May you be well.
May you be peaceful
and at ease. May
you be happy.*

———

ANONYMOUS

9

JANUARY

Enthusiasm is the electricity of life. How do you get it? You act enthusiastic until you make it a habit.

———

GORDON PARKS, PHOTOGRAPHER

10
JANUARY

Happiness. Simple as a glass of chocolate or tortuous as the heart. Bitter. Sweet. Alive.

JOANNE HARRIS, AUTHOR

11
JANUARY

A desk is a dangerous place from which to view the world.

JOHN LE CARRÉ, AUTHOR

If there is at least one person you've helped in life, then your life has been worthwhile.

L. SYDNEY ABEL, AUTHOR

13

JANUARY

Above all else, guard
your heart for it
affects everything
else you do.

ANONYMOUS

14

JANUARY

There is a certain enthusiasm in liberty, that makes human nature rise above itself, in acts of bravery and heroism.

ALEXANDER HAMILTON, U.S. FOUNDING FATHER

15

JANUARY

Everyone knows that ice cream is worth the trouble of being cold. Like all things virtuous, you have to suffer to gain the reward.

———

BRANDON SANDERSON, AUTHOR

16

JANUARY

We can know only
that we know
nothing. And that is
the highest degree
of human wisdom.

LEO TOLSTOY, AUTHOR

17
JANUARY

I am convinced that life is 10% what happens to me and 90% how I react to it. And so it is with you. . . . We are in charge of our attitudes.

———

CHARLES R. SWINDOLL, PASTOR

18

*Darkness cannot drive
out darkness:
only light can do that.
Hate cannot drive out hate:
only love can do that.*

———

MARTIN LUTHER KING JR.,
CIVIL RIGHTS ACTIVIST

19

JANUARY

THERE IS A TIME FOR WORDS AND A TIME FOR SLEEP.

———

HOMER, AUTHOR

20
JANUARY

THE EARLY BIRD GETS THE WORM, BUT THE SECOND MOUSE GETS THE CHEESE.

ANONYMOUS

21
JANUARY

You can't fix things with a hug, but you can't make them any worse, either.

DEAN KOONTZ, AUTHOR

The clouds above us
join and separate,
The breeze in the courtyard
leaves and returns.
Life is like that,
so why not relax?
Who can stop us from
celebrating?

———

LU YU, THE SAGE OF TEA

23
JANUARY

Make a fist. Lightly.
Leave enough room
for a breath to pass
through. Good.
Good. All magic
proceeds from breath.
Remember that.

———

CLIVE BARKER, AUTHOR

24
JANUARY

My life amounts to no
more than one drop in
a limitless ocean. Yet
what is any ocean, but
a multitude of drops?

DAVID MITCHELL, AUTHOR

It is very rare or almost impossible that an event can be negative from all points of view.

DALAI LAMA, BUDDHIST MONK

26

IT'S AMAZING HOW A LITTLE TOMORROW CAN MAKE UP FOR A WHOLE LOT OF YESTERDAY.

JOHN GUARE, PLAYWRIGHT

Strength is the capacity
to break a Hershey bar
into four pieces with your
bare hands—and then eat
just one of the pieces.

———

JUDITH VIORST, AUTHOR

28
JANUARY

Choose a job you
love, and you will
never have to work
a day in your life.

———

ANONYMOUS

The world's a puzzle; no need to make sense out of it.

SOCRATES, PHILOSOPHER

After all, there are no mistakes in life, only lessons.

LYNDA RENHAM, AUTHOR

31

JANUARY

Someday this upside-down
world will be turned right-side
up. Nothing in all eternity will
turn it back again. If we are
wise, we will use our brief
lives on earth positioning
ourselves for the turn.

———

RANDY ALCORN, AUTHOR

1

FEBRUARY

Lock up your
libraries if you like;
but there is no gate,
no lock, no bolt
that you can set
upon the freedom
of my mind.

———

VIRGINIA WOOLF, AUTHOR

2
FEBRUARY

To wish to be young again and to have the benefit of one's learned and acquired existence is not at all to wish for a repeat performance, or a Groundhog Day.

———

CHRISTOPHER HITCHENS, AUTHOR

3

FEBRUARY

*Music is the great uniter.
An incredible force.
Something that people
who differ on everything
and anything else can
have in common.*

SARAH DESSEN, AUTHOR

4

FEBRUARY

Some quick
advice for
success in life:
Don't be afraid,
be amazing.

DR. CUTHBERT SOUP, AUTHOR

5

FEBRUARY

From where we stand the rain seems random. If we could stand somewhere else, we would see the order in it.

TONY HILLERMAN, AUTHOR

6

FEBRUARY

Be like a duck, paddling and
working very hard inside the
water, but what everyone sees
is a smiling and calm face.

———

MANOJ ARORA, AUTHOR

7

FEBRUARY

Don't walk in front of me . . .
I may not follow
Don't walk behind me . . .
I may not lead
Walk beside me . . .
just be my friend.

———

ANONYMOUS

8

FEBRUARY

A KITE ONLY FLIES IF IT'S TETHERED.

VICTOR ROBERT LEE, AUTHOR

9

FEBRUARY

TRUE LOVE IS LIKE LITTLE ROSES, SWEET, FRAGRANT IN SMALL DOSES.

ANA CLAUDIA ANTUNES, AUTHOR

10

FEBRUARY

We dream to give
ourselves hope. To
stop dreaming—well,
that's like saying
you can never
change your fate.

———

AMY TAN, AUTHOR

11
FEBRUARY

When you do talk to people, share what you are. Stop focusing on all the things that you aren't.

DAN PEARCE, AUTHOR

Always bear in mind that your own resolution to succeed is more important than any other one thing.

ABRAHAM LINCOLN, U.S. PRESIDENT

13

FEBRUARY

Curiosity is one of the permanent and certain characteristics of a vigorous intellect.

———

SAMUEL JOHNSON, AUTHOR

14

FEBRUARY

*And so let us always
meet each other with
a smile, for the smile is
the beginning of love.*

———

MOTHER TERESA, CATHOLIC MISSIONARY

15

FEBRUARY

BELIEVE YOU CAN AND YOU'RE HALFWAY THERE.

THEODORE ROOSEVELT, U.S. PRESIDENT

16
FEBRUARY

If you're not having fun, you're doing something wrong.

GROUCHO MARX, COMEDIAN

17

FEBRUARY

Through Compassion and Care we are compelled to random acts of kindness and demonstrations of love.

———

JEAN HAMILTON-FORD, AUTHOR

18
FEBRUARY

Accept what life offers you and try to drink from every cup. All wines should be tasted; some should only be sipped, but with others, drink the whole bottle.

PAULO COELHO, AUTHOR

A PERSON WHO NEVER MADE A MISTAKE NEVER TRIED ANYTHING NEW.

ALBERT EINSTEIN, PHYSICIST

20
FEBRUARY

What matters most is how well you walk through the fire.

CHARLES BUKOWSKI, POET

21

FEBRUARY

The smell of good bread
baking, like the sound of
lightly flowing water, is
indescribable in its evocation
of innocence and delight.

———

M.F.K. FISHER, FOOD WRITER

Do not spoil what you have by desiring what you have not; remember that what you now have was once among the things you only hoped for.

EPICURUS, PHILOSOPHER

23
FEBRUARY

TRULY HAPPY MEMORIES ALWAYS LIVE ON, SHINING. OVER TIME, ONE BY ONE, THEY COME BACK TO LIFE.

BANANA YOSHIMOTO, AUTHOR

24

FEBRUARY

There are always surprises. Life
may be inveterately grim and
the surprises disproportionately
unpleasant, but it would be
hardly worth living if there were
no exceptions, no sunny days,
no acts of random kindness.

T. C. BOYLE, AUTHOR

25

FEBRUARY

I have always thirsted for knowledge, I have always been full of questions.

———

HERMANN HESSE, AUTHOR

26
FEBRUARY

THERE ARE MANY KINDS OF JOY, BUT THEY ALL LEAD TO ONE: THE JOY TO BE LOVED.

MICHAEL ENDE, AUTHOR

27
FEBRUARY

Scared is what you're feeling. Brave is what you're doing.

———

EMMA DONOGHUE, AUTHOR

28
FEBRUARY

Each night, when
I go to sleep, I die.
And the next morning,
when I wake up,
I am reborn.

MAHATMA GANDHI, ACTIVIST

I'm taking the leap, I'm learning to fly.

NIHAR SHARMA, AUTHOR

1

MARCH

One way to
remember who
you are is to
remember who
your heroes are.

———

STEVE JOBS, COFOUNDER OF APPLE INC.

2

MARCH

Books are the ultimate
Dumpees: put them down and
they'll wait for you forever;
pay attention to them and
they always love you back.

———

JOHN GREEN, AUTHOR

3

MARCH

The beautiful journey of today can only begin when we learn to let go of yesterday.

DR. STEVE MARABOLI, BEHAVIORAL SCIENTIST

4
MARCH

NEVER ACCEPT LIMITATIONS.

JAKE BYRNE, ATHLETE

5
MARCH

I hold that a strongly marked
personality can influence
descendants for generations.

———

BEATRIX POTTER, AUTHOR

6
MARCH

*I've never met
a problem a
proper cupcake
couldn't fix.*

SARAH OCKLER, AUTHOR

7

MARCH

If we can share our
story with someone
who responds
with empathy and
understanding,
shame can't survive.

BRENÉ BROWN, AUTHOR

8

MARCH

The road that is built in hope is
more pleasant to the traveler
than the road built in despair,
even though they both lead
to the same destination.

———

MARION ZIMMER BRADLEY, AUTHOR

9
MARCH

Revolution begins with the self, in the self.

TONI CADE BAMBARA, AUTHOR AND ACTIVIST

You are the sky.
Everything
else it's just the
weather.

PEMA CHÖDRÖN, BUDDHIST
TEACHER AND AUTHOR

11

MARCH

It's best to have your tools with you. If you don't, you're apt to find something you didn't expect and get discouraged.

STEPHEN KING, AUTHOR

12

MARCH

Don't be ashamed to weep;
'tis right to grieve. Tears
are only water, and flowers,
trees, and fruit cannot
grow without water.

———

BRIAN JACQUES, AUTHOR

13
MARCH

Not everyone is your brother or sister in the faith, but everyone is your neighbor, and you must love your neighbor.

TIMOTHY KELLER, PASTOR

14
MARCH

THINKING VERY OFTEN RESEMBLES NAPPING, BUT THE INTENT IS DIFFERENT.

JANET EVANOVICH, AUTHOR

15
MARCH

The soil is the great connector
of lives, the source and
destination of all. It is the healer
and restorer and resurrector,
by which disease passes into
health, age into youth, death
into life. Without proper care for
it we can have no community,
because without proper care
for it we can have no life.

WENDELL BERRY, AUTHOR

It is a capital mistake to theorize before one has data. Insensibly one begins to twist facts to suit theories, instead of theories to suit facts.

SIR ARTHUR CONAN DOYLE, AUTHOR

17
MARCH

St. Patrick's Day
is an enchanted
time—a day to
begin transforming
winter's dreams into
summer's magic.

ANONYMOUS

18
MARCH

*There are so many ways
to be brave in this world.
Sometimes bravery
involves laying down
your life for something
bigger than yourself,
or for someone else.*

———

VERONICA ROTH, AUTHOR

19

MARCH

Life is worth living as long as there's a laugh in it.

———

L. M. MONTGOMERY, AUTHOR

I can still bring into my body
the joy I felt at seeing the first
trillium of spring, which seemed
to be telling me, "Never give
up hope, spring will come."

———

JESSICA STERN, AUTHOR

21
MARCH

As we are, so we
do; and as we do,
so is it done to us;
we are the builders
of our fortunes.

———

RALPH WALDO EMERSON, AUTHOR

22
MARCH

THE PAST IS ALWAYS TENSE, THE FUTURE PERFECT.

—

ZADIE SMITH, AUTHOR

23
MARCH

You come into this world alone and die alone, but there's a really long stretch in the middle that can be extraordinarily meaningful and even fun with the right people. And when it's not fun, they'll be with you, too.

JULIE KLAM, AUTHOR

24
MARCH

Your harshest critic is
always going to be yourself.
Don't ignore that critic but
don't give it more attention
than it deserves.

———

MICHAEL IAN BLACK, COMEDIAN

25
MARCH

NOT ALL THOSE WHO WANDER ARE LOST.

———

J.R.R. TOLKIEN, AUTHOR

26
MARCH

Life is indeed colorful. We can feel in the pink one day, with our bank balances comfortably in the black, and the grass seemingly no greener on the other side of the fence. Then out of the blue, something tiresome happens that makes us see red, turn ashen white, even purple with rage. Maybe controlling our varying emotions is just "color management" by another name.

ALEX MORRITT, AUTHOR

27

MARCH

Things happen, and nothing is for sure, but you just have to keep going, believing that one day, you'll find something that is.

———

A. J. DARKHOLME, AUTHOR

28
MARCH

THE MOST BASIC WAY TO GET SOMEONE'S ATTENTION IS THIS: BREAK A PATTERN.

CHIP HEATH AND DAN HEATH, AUTHORS

29
MARCH

Yesterday is but a dream,
Tomorrow is only a vision.
But today well lived makes
every yesterday
a dream of happiness,
and every tomorrow
a vision of hope.

KALIDASA, POET

30
MARCH

Home is everything you can walk to.

―――

JERRY SPINELLI, AUTHOR

31
MARCH

AND THERE'S NO SUCH THING AS TOO MUCH BACKUP.

TERRY PRATCHETT AND
STEPHEN BAXTER, AUTHORS

1
APRIL

Any fool can make a rule And any fool will mind it.

HENRY DAVID THOREAU, AUTHOR

2
APRIL

If there is to be reconciliation, first there must be truth.

TIMOTHY B. TYSON, AUTHOR

3

APRIL

Life throws challenges
and every challenge
comes with rainbows and
lights to conquer it.

———

AMIT RAY, AUTHOR

4

APRIL

That perfect tranquility of life, which is nowhere to be found but in retreat, a faithful friend, and a good library.

———

APHRA BEHN, POET

I think love is caramel. Sweet
and fragrant; always welcome.
It is the gentle golden color
of a setting harvest sun; the
warmth of a squeezed embrace;
the easy melting of two souls
into one and a taste that
lingers even when everything
else has melted away. Once
tasted it is never forgotten.

———

JENNY COLGAN, AUTHOR

And human will is the strongest force ever created. There are those born to succeed and those who are determined to succeed. The former fall into it, and the latter pursue it all costs. They won't be denied. Nothing daunts them.

SHERRILYN KENYON, AUTHOR

7

APRIL

It's high time you
were shown that
you really don't
know all there is
to be known.

———

DR. SEUSS, AUTHOR

Life is so beautiful that death has fallen in love with it, a jealous, possessive love that grabs at what it can.

YANN MARTEL, AUTHOR

THE POSITIVE THINKER SEES THE INVISIBLE, FEELS THE INTANGIBLE, AND ACHIEVES THE IMPOSSIBLE.

———

WINSTON CHURCHILL, BRITISH PRIME MINISTER

10
APRIL

Some people grumble that roses have thorns; I am grateful that thorns have roses.

———

ALPHONSE KARR, AUTHOR

11
APRIL

No one saves us but ourselves.
No one can and no one may. We
ourselves must walk the path.

———

GAUTAMA BUDDHA, BUDDHIST SAGE

12
APRIL

Friendship is the best kind of ship.

JENNIFER LANE, AUTHOR

13
APRIL

When angry count to ten before you speak. If very angry, count to one hundred.

THOMAS JEFFERSON, U.S. PRESIDENT

14
APRIL

Keep a little fire burning; however small, however hidden.

CORMAC MCCARTHY, AUTHOR

I have learned all
kinds of things from
my many mistakes.
The one thing I
never learn is to
stop making them.

JOE ABERCROMBIE, AUTHOR

Sunsets, like childhood, are viewed with wonder not just because they are beautiful but because they are fleeting.

———

RICHARD PAUL EVANS, AUTHOR

17
APRIL

Remember, remember always
that all of us, and you and I
especially, are descended from
immigrants and revolutionists.

FRANKLIN D. ROOSEVELT, U.S. PRESIDENT

18
APRIL

DOGS MAKE GREAT SHRINKS. NO JUDGMENT, NO CO-PAYMENT.

ANDI BROWN, AUTHOR

19
APRIL

When someone steals another's clothes, we call them a thief. Should we not give the same name to one who could clothe the naked and does not?

BASIL OF CAESAREA, SAINT

The world turns on our every action, and our every omission, whether we know it or not.

———

ABRAHAM VERGHESE, PHYSICIAN

21
APRIL

It doesn't matter
what you say
you believe—
it only matters
what you do.

ROBERT FULGHUM, AUTHOR

PASSOVER IS A LIVING PICTURE OF HOW SALVATION IS PROPERLY OBTAINED, AS WE SHALL SEE.

ZOLA LEVITT, MINISTER

23
APRIL

A picnic is more than eating a meal; it is a pleasurable state of mind.

DEEDEE STOVEL, AUTHOR

24
APRIL

There will always be detours in the fascinating game called life. Find the path to your heart's desires, and stay on course.

ELIZABETH PARKER, AUTHOR

25
APRIL

A kiss is a secret which takes the lips for the ear.

EDMOND ROSTAND, POET

26
APRIL

A true conservationist is a man
who knows that the world is
not given by his fathers, but
borrowed from his children.

———

JOHN JAMES AUDUBON, NATURALIST

27
APRIL

The world is a book and those who do not travel read only one page.

AUGUSTINE OF HIPPO, SAINT

28
APRIL

Poetry is a mirror which makes beautiful that which is distorted.

———

PERCY BYSSHE SHELLEY, POET

THE BEST TIME TO PLANT A TREE WAS 20 YEARS AGO. THE NEXT BEST TIME IS NOW.

CHINESE PROVERB

30
APRIL

Be yourself; everyone else is already taken.

OSCAR WILDE, AUTHOR

1

MAY

*We have to recognize
that there cannot be
relationships unless there
is commitment, unless there
is loyalty, unless there is
love, patience, persistence.*

BELL HOOKS AND CORNEL WEST, AUTHORS

2
MAY

Art is unquestionably one
of the purest and highest
elements in human happiness.
It trains the mind through
the eye, and the eye through
the mind. As the sun colors
flowers, so does art color life.

JOHN LUBBOCK, SCIENTIST

3
MAY

I am no bird; and no
net ensnares me: I am a
free human being with
an independent will.

———

CHARLOTTE BRONTË, AUTHOR

4

MAY

MAY THE FORCE BE WITH YOU.

STAR WARS, EPISODE IV: A NEW HOPE

5
MAY

Faith lightens the
path your shadowed
mind has to walk.

MICHELLE HORST, AUTHOR

6
MAY

*Drink because you are
happy, but never because
you are miserable.*

———

G. K. CHESTERTON, AUTHOR

7
MAY

There is only what you want
and what happens. There is
only grabbing on and holding
tight in the darkness.

LAUREN OLIVER, AUTHOR

8

MAY

God could not
be everywhere,
and therefore he
made mothers.

———

JEWISH PROVERB

9

MAY

If you want to know what a man's like, take a good look at how he treats his inferiors, not his equals.

J. K. ROWLING, AUTHOR

10
MAY

Once you have mastered a technique, you hardly need look at a recipe again, and can take off on your own.

———

JULIA CHILD, CHEF

THERE WAS NOTHING IN THE DARK THAT WASN'T THERE WHEN THE LIGHTS WERE ON.

ROD SERLING, SCREENWRITER

12
MAY

Mediocrity is always in a rush; but whatever is worth doing at all is worth doing with consideration.

AMELIA EDITH HUDDLESTON BARR, AUTHOR

13

MAY

Curb your fretting,
tadpole, or the frog
of your future will
fail to croak.

———

PAUL COLLINS, AUTHOR

14
MAY

*If love be blind,
love cannot hit
the mark.*

———

WILLIAM SHAKESPEARE, PLAYWRIGHT

15
MAY

And I will never again underestimate the power of anticipation. There is no better boost in the present than an invitation into the future.

CAROLINE KEPNES, AUTHOR

16
MAY

To be poor and be without trees, is to be the most starved human being in the world. To be poor and have trees, is to be completely rich in ways that money can never buy.

CLARISSA PINKOLA ESTÉS, AUTHOR

17
MAY

OLD AGE IS A WONDERFUL DISGUISE.

KATHERINE APPLEGATE, AUTHOR

18
MAY

Things end. People leave. And
you know what? Life goes on.
Besides, if bad things didn't
happen, how would you be
able to feel the good ones?

———

ELIZABETH SCOTT, AUTHOR

19
MAY

Keep your face to the sun and you will never see the shadows.

HELEN KELLER, AUTHOR AND ACTIVIST

20
MAY

Life is no different than the weather. Not only is it unpredictable, but it shows us a new perspective of the world every day.

———

SUZY KASSEM, AUTHOR

21
MAY

THE WATER DOESN'T KNOW HOW OLD YOU ARE.

DARA TORRES, OLYMPIC GOLD MEDALIST

22
MAY

Every single day I'll
keep you with me,
no matter how far
from me you are.

———

S. C. STEPHENS, AUTHOR

What do you do with all
your pennies? I give them
away. It's good to spread
your luck around and it
always comes back to you.

———

FANNIE FLAGG, ACTOR

24
MAY

Even a snail will
eventually reach
its destination.

GAIL TSUKIYAMA, AUTHOR

25
MAY

A woman with confidence is hypnotic. A smile is mesmerizing. Presence, openness, a sense of humor these are all things that make a woman attractive.

JESSICA ORTNER, AUTHOR

26
MAY

Sometimes you have to work hard for what you want. Sometimes, hard work is what makes it precious.

UTE CARBONE, AUTHOR

27
MAY

I cannot say whether things
will get better if we change;
what I can say is that they must
change if they are to get better.

———

GEORG CHRISTOPH LICHTENBERG, SCIENTIST

28
MAY

IT'S TIME TO START LIVING THE LIFE YOU'VE IMAGINED.

HENRY JAMES, AUTHOR

29
MAY

*Just as when we come
into the world, when
we die we are afraid of
unknown things. But the
fear is something from
within us that has nothing
to do with reality.*

———

ISABEL ALLENDE, AUTHOR

30
MAY

I have to live if I want to be remembered.

SUZANNE YOUNG, AUTHOR

31
MAY

The art of
conversation is
the art of hearing
as well as of
being heard.

WILLIAM HAZLITT, ESSAYIST

1

PAIN IS INEVITABLE. SUFFERING IS OPTIONAL.

HARUKI MURAKAMI, AUTHOR

2

JUNE

Be steady and
well-ordered in your
life so that you can
be fierce and original
in your work.

———

GUSTAVE FLAUBERT, AUTHOR

3
JUNE

I want all of us to move into the future with hope and with the spirit of oneness and unity.

JOYCE BANDA, POLITICIAN

4
JUNE

Through pain I've learned to comfort suffering men.

VIRGIL, POET

5

JUNE

It's one thing knowing you have people cheering you on, yet another to know they have walked in your footsteps.

———

CHRISTINE MAGNUS MOORE, AUTHOR

6
JUNE

In the future, there will be no female leaders. There will just be leaders.

SHERYL SANDBERG, TECHNOLOGY EXECUTIVE

7

JUNE

Patience is a conquering virtue.

GEOFFREY CHAUCER, POET

THAT WAS WHAT A
BEST FRIEND DID:
HOLD UP A MIRROR
AND SHOW YOU
YOUR HEART.

KRISTIN HANNAH, AUTHOR

9
JUNE

If you retain nothing
else, always remember
the most important
rule of beauty.
Who cares?

———

TINA FEY, COMEDIAN

10
JUNE

Be clearly aware of the
stars and infinity on high.
Then life seems almost
enchanted after all.

———

VINCENT VAN GOGH, PAINTER

11

JUNE

*It's hard to beat
a person who
never gives up.*

———

BABE RUTH, ATHLETE

12
JUNE

WHAT WE PLAY IS LIFE.

LOUIS ARMSTRONG, MUSICIAN

13
JUNE

Positive anything
is better than
negative nothing.

———

ELBERT HUBBARD, AUTHOR

14
JUNE

If you talk about it, it's a dream, if you envision it, it's possible, but if you schedule it, it's real.

———

ANTHONY ROBBINS, MOTIVATIONAL SPEAKER

It may be normal, darling; but I'd rather be natural.

TRUMAN CAPOTE, AUTHOR

16
JUNE

NO GROUP PICTURE IS GOING TO HAVE THE POWER OF AN INDIVIDUAL PORTRAIT.

ANNIE LEIBOVITZ, PHOTOGRAPHER

Sometimes you just have to bite your upper lip and put sunglasses on.

BOB DYLAN, MUSICIAN

18

JUNE

Whatever you choose, however many roads you travel, I hope that you choose not to be a lady. I hope you will find some way to break the rules and make a little trouble out there. And I also hope that you will choose to make some of that trouble on behalf of women.

———

NORA EPHRON, AUTHOR

19
JUNE

It was times like these when I thought my father, who hated guns and had never been to any wars, was the bravest man who ever lived.

HARPER LEE, AUTHOR

20
JUNE

Don't think the
summer is over,
even when roses
droop and turn
brown and the
stars shift position
in the sky.

———

ALICE HOFFMAN, AUTHOR

YOU HAVE TO BE ABLE TO RECOGNIZE YOUR TRUTHS IN THE DAYLIGHT BEFORE YOU CAN FIND THEM IN THE DARK.

KELLI JAE BAELI, AUTHOR

22
JUNE

Don't tell me how educated you are, tell me how much you have traveled.

———

THE QURAN

23

JUNE

You might be poor,
your shoes might
be broken, but your
mind is a palace.

———

FRANK MCCOURT, AUTHOR

24
JUNE

THE UNIVERSE DOESN'T ALLOW PERFECTION.

STEPHEN HAWKING, PHYSICIST

25

JUNE

Like I'm always telling my brothers, if you gonna go into history, you can't do it with a hate attitude.

———

DEBORAH LACKS, AS QUOTED IN *THE IMMORTAL LIFE OF HENRIETTA LACKS*

26
JUNE

Hard work is only a prison sentence when you lack motivation.

MALCOLM GLADWELL, AUTHOR

I prefer to be true to myself, even at the hazard of incurring the ridicule of others, rather than to be false, and to incur my own abhorrence.

FREDERICK DOUGLASS, SOCIAL ACTIVIST

28
JUNE

What you believe has more
power than what you dream
or wish or hope for. You
become what you believe.

———

OPRAH WINFREY, MEDIA PERSONALITY

Not everything has to have a point. Some things just are.

———

JUDY BLUME, AUTHOR

30
JUNE

The more people that meet each other, the better it is for all of them.

―――

L. SPRAGUE DE CAMP AND
FLETCHER PRATT, AUTHORS

1

JULY

I HAVE LEARNED THAT TO BE WITH THOSE I LIKE IS ENOUGH.

WALT WHITMAN, POET

2

JULY

One touch of nature makes the whole world kin.

———

JOHN MUIR, NATURALIST

3

JULY

Good ideas are always crazy until they're not.

———

ELON MUSK, INVENTOR

4
JULY

INDEPENDENCE IS MY HAPPINESS, THE WORLD IS MY COUNTRY, AND MY RELIGION IS TO DO GOOD.

THOMAS PAYNE, POLITICAL ACTIVIST

5
JULY

Concentrate all
your thoughts upon
the work in hand.
The sun's rays
do not burn until
brought to a focus.

ALEXANDER GRAHAM BELL, INVENTOR

6

JULY

They always say that time changes things, but you actually have to change them yourself.

———

ANDY WARHOL, ARTIST

7

JULY

A man's daughter is his
heart. Just with feet,
walking out in the world.

———

MAT JOHNSON, AUTHOR

8

JULY

It does not take many words to tell the truth.

SITTING BULL, LAKOTA CHIEF

9

JULY

Please don't be offended if I preach to you a while, Tears are out of place in eyes that were meant to smile.

—

BUD DESYLVA, SONGWRITER

10
JULY

Have a heart that
never hardens, and
a temper that never
tires, and a touch
that never hurts.

―――――

CHARLES DICKENS, AUTHOR

11
JULY

LOVE IS A GOOD THING ON A BAD DAY, WHEN THE LAST THING YOU WANT IS TO BE CHEERED UP.

CHAD SUGG, MUSICIAN

12
JULY

One day I will find
the right words, and
they will be simple.

JACK KEROUAC, AUTHOR

13
JULY

Definitions belong to the definers, not the defined.

———

TONI MORRISON, AUTHOR

14
JULY

*A Nation should not
be judged by how it
treats its highest citizens,
but its lowest ones.*

NELSON MANDELA, PRESIDENT
OF SOUTH AFRICA

15
JULY

You give but little when you
give of your possessions.
It is when you give of
yourself that you truly give.

———

KAHLIL GIBRAN, AUTHOR

16
JULY

IF I'M SINCERE TODAY, WHAT DOES IT MATTER IF I REGRET IT TOMORROW?

JOSÉ SARAMAGO, AUTHOR

17

JULY

Life is better than death, I believe, if only because it is less boring . . .

———

ALICE WALKER, AUTHOR

18
JULY

*When you stare
at someone long
enough, you discover
their humanity.*

———

AS GOOD AS IT GETS

19
JULY

Perfection is
not attainable,
but if we chase
perfection we can
catch excellence.

VINCE LOMBARDI, ATHLETE

20
JULY

I'm in no hurry: the sun and
the moon aren't, either.
Nobody goes faster than the
legs they have. If where I
want to go is far away, I'm
not there in an instant.

————

FERNANDO PESSOA AS ALBERTO CAEIRO, POET

21

JULY

The only way we will survive is by being kind. The only way we can get by in this world is through the help we receive from others. No one can do it alone, no matter how great the machines are.

AMY POEHLER, COMEDIAN

22
JULY

I beg you take courage; the brave soul can mend even disaster.

CATHERINE THE GREAT, RULER OF RUSSIA

23
JULY

I would like to be
remembered, well . . . the
Mexicans have a phrase,
Feo fuerte y formal. Which
means he was ugly,
strong, and had dignity.

———

JOHN WAYNE, ACTOR

PARENTHOOD ... IT'S ABOUT GUIDING THE NEXT GENERATION, AND FORGIVING THE LAST.

PETER KRAUSE, ACTOR

25
JULY

Life isn't a merry-go-round,
it's a roller coaster.
Life won't always be smooth,
it may not always be pretty,
but it will be an adventure—
one not to be missed.

———

ROBERT A. GLOVER, AUTHOR

Hope makes a good breakfast. Eat plenty of it.

IAN FLEMING, AUTHOR

27
JULY

Just because a man lacks the use of his eyes doesn't mean he lacks vision.

STEVIE WONDER, MUSICIAN

28
JULY

When an enemy praises an enemy, the smart man listens.

BUFFALO SOLDIERS

A LITTLE NONSENSE NOW AND THEN, IS RELISHED BY THE WISEST MEN.

ROALD DAHL, AUTHOR

30
JULY

Never to suffer would never to have been blessed.

———

EDGAR ALLAN POE, AUTHOR

31
JULY

People think a soul mate is your perfect fit, and that's what everyone wants. But a true soul mate is a mirror, the person who shows you everything that is holding you back, the person who brings you to your own attention so you can change your life.

———

ELIZABETH GILBERT, AUTHOR

1

AUGUST

People can tell you to
keep your mouth shut, but
it doesn't stop you from
having your own opinion.

———

ANNE FRANK, DIARIST

2

AUGUST

Never be bored, and you will never be boring.

ELEANOR ROOSEVELT, DIPLOMAT AND ACTIVIST

Carry out a random act of kindness with no expectation of reward, safe in the knowledge that one day someone might do the same for you.

———

DIANA, PRINCESS OF WALES

Anyone with gumption and a sharp mind will take the measure of two things: what's said and what's done.

BEOWULF

5
AUGUST

AS COAL PRESSURED INTO PEARLS BY OUR WEIGHTY EXISTENCE. BEAUTY THAT AROSE OUT OF PAIN.

———

SUZANNE COLLINS, AUTHOR

6

AUGUST

Individually, every grain of sand brushing against my hands represents a story, an experience, and a block for me to build upon for the next generation.

———

RAQUEL CEPEDA, JOURNALIST

7

And now here is my secret, a very simple secret: It is only with the heart that one can see rightly; what is essential is invisible to the eye.

———

ANTOINE DE SAINT-EXUPÉRY, AUTHOR

8

AUGUST

Life is so much richer, so very much more meaningful, if you plant yourself in a place that will nourish you.

———

ANN SHAYNE, AUTHOR

THINK BEFORE YOU SPEAK. READ BEFORE YOU THINK.

———

FRAN LEBOWITZ, AUTHOR

10
AUGUST

We often miss opportunity because it's dressed in overalls and looks like work.

———

THOMAS EDISON, INVENTOR

11
AUGUST

We need to remember across generations that there is as much to learn as there is to teach.

GLORIA STEINEM, FEMINIST AUTHOR

LET US LEARN TO SHOW OUR FRIENDSHIP FOR A MAN WHEN HE IS ALIVE AND NOT AFTER HE IS DEAD.

F. SCOTT FITZGERALD, AUTHOR

Others have seen what is and asked why. I have seen what could be and asked why not.

PABLO PICASSO, PAINTER

14
AUGUST

One of the things my parents
taught me, and I'll always be
grateful for the gift, is to not
ever let anybody else define me;
that for me to define myself.

———

WILMA MANKILLER, CHEROKEE CHIEF

15

AUGUST

Keep your best wishes, close to your heart and watch what happens.

TONY DELISO, AUTHOR

CHANCE RUNS LIKE A RIVER THROUGH ALL OUR LIVES, AND BEING PREPARED FOR SURPRISE IS THE BEST WE CAN DO.

KENNETH OPPEL, AUTHOR

Think you're escaping and run into yourself. Longest way round is the shortest way home.

———

JAMES JOYCE, AUTHOR

18
AUGUST

For, while the tale of how we suffer, and how we are delighted, and how we may triumph is never new, it always must be heard.

JAMES BALDWIN, AUTHOR

19
AUGUST

The more one does and sees and feels, the more one is able to do, and the more genuine may be one's appreciation of fundamental things like home, and love, and understanding companionship.

———

AMELIA EARHART, AVIATOR

20
AUGUST

Memories remind us that every moment of our lives, even the most tragic, has contributed to our strength. We've gotten through. We're still here.

———

WILLIE NELSON, MUSICIAN

21
AUGUST

I am incapable of conceiving
infinity, and yet I do not accept
finity. I want this adventure
that is the context of my
life to go on without end.

———

SIMONE DE BEAUVOIR, FEMINIST THEORIST

22
AUGUST

THE GREATEST SELF IS A PEACEFUL SMILE, THAT ALWAYS SEES THE WORLD SMILING BACK.

BRYANT MCGILL AND JENNI YOUNG, AUTHORS

23

AUGUST

It's the questions we can't answer that teach us the most. They teach us how to think. If you give a man an answer, all he gains is a little fact. But give him a question and he'll look for his own answers.

PATRICK ROTHFUSS, AUTHOR

24
AUGUST

And now these
three remain: faith,
hope, and love.
But the greatest
of these is love.

———

THE BIBLE

25
AUGUST

To err is human, to forgive, divine.

ALEXANDER POPE, POET

*I do not wish [women]
to have power over men;
but over themselves.*

———

MARY WOLLSTONECRAFT, AUTHOR

27

AUGUST

Sometimes the hardest part
isn't letting go but rather
learning to start over.

———

NICOLE SOBON, AUTHOR

28
AUGUST

It is better to be hated for what you are than to be loved for what you are not.

ANDRÉ GIDE, AUTHOR

I MAY NOT HAVE GONE WHERE I INTENDED TO GO, BUT I THINK I HAVE ENDED UP WHERE I NEEDED TO BE.

———

DOUGLAS ADAMS, AUTHOR

30
AUGUST

If you remain calm in the midst of great chaos, it is the surest guarantee that it will eventually subside.

JULIE ANDREWS, ACTOR

31
AUGUST

Dreams are lovely. But they are just dreams. Fleeting, ephemeral, pretty. But dreams do not come true just because you dream them. It's hard work that makes things happen. It's hard work that creates change.

SHONDA RHIMES, SCREENWRITER

1
SEPTEMBER

Never let the future disturb you. You will meet it, if you have to, with the same weapons of reason which today arm you against the present.

———

MARCUS AURELIUS, ROMAN EMPEROR

2

SEPTEMBER

I disapprove of what you say, but I will defend to the death your right to say it.

S. G. TALLENTYRE, AUTHOR

3
SEPTEMBER

IT HAS ALWAYS BEEN EASY TO HATE AND DESTROY. TO BUILD AND TO CHERISH IS MUCH MORE DIFFICULT.

QUEEN ELIZABETH II

4

SEPTEMBER

Clouds come floating into my life, no longer to carry rain or usher storm, but to add color to my sunset sky.

—

RABINDRANATH TAGORE, AUTHOR

He who works with his
hands is a laborer.
He who works with
his hands and his head
is a craftsman.
He who works with his
hands and his head and
his heart is an artist.

———

FRANCIS OF ASSISI, SAINT

6
SEPTEMBER

Today I choose life. Every
morning when I wake up I
can choose joy, happiness,
negativity, pain. . . .To feel
the freedom that comes from
being able to continue to make
mistakes and choices—today I
choose to feel life, not to deny
my humanity but embrace it.

———

KEVYN AUCOIN, MAKEUP ARTIST

7
SEPTEMBER

Fall has always been my favorite season. The time when everything bursts with its last beauty, as if nature had been saving up all year for the grand finale.

———

LAUREN DESTEFANO, AUTHOR

8

SEPTEMBER

How beautiful the world would
be if there were a procedure
for moving through labyrinths.

———

UMBERTO ECO, AUTHOR

9

SEPTEMBER

To understand all is to forgive all.

EVELYN WAUGH, AUTHOR

10
SEPTEMBER

BE LESS CURIOUS ABOUT PEOPLE AND MORE CURIOUS ABOUT IDEAS.

MARIE CURIE, CHEMIST

11
SEPTEMBER

Remember the hours after
September 11 when we came
together as one. . . . It was
the worst day we have
ever seen, but it brought
out the best in all of us.

———

JOHN KERRY, U.S. SENATOR

12
SEPTEMBER

Your conscience is the measure of the honesty of your selfishness. Listen to it carefully.

RICHARD BACH, AUTHOR

*It's special, grandparents
and grandchildren. . . .
Gone are the bonds of
guilt and responsibility
that burden the maternal
relationship. The way
to love is free.*

———

KATE MORTON, AUTHOR

14
SEPTEMBER

If you treat an individual as he is, he will remain how he is. But if you treat him as if he were what he ought to be and could be, he will become what he ought to be and could be.

JOHANN WOLFGANG VON GOETHE, AUTHOR

15
SEPTEMBER

In politics as in philosophy, my tenets are few and simple. The leading one of which, and indeed that which embraces most others, is to be honest and just ourselves and to exact it from others.

GEORGE WASHINGTON, U.S. PRESIDENT

16
SEPTEMBER

THERE ARE YEARS THAT ASK QUESTIONS AND YEARS THAT ANSWER.

———

ZORA NEALE HURSTON, AUTHOR

17
SEPTEMBER

You can't wait for inspiration. You have to go after it with a club.

JACK LONDON, AUTHOR

18

SEPTEMBER

The soul is healed by being with children.

FYODOR DOSTOYEVSKY, AUTHOR

19
SEPTEMBER

There is no dishonor in
losing the race. There is only
dishonor in not racing because
you are afraid to lose.

———

GARTH STEIN, AUTHOR

We are not simply in the
universe, we are part of it.
We are born from it. One
might even say we have been
empowered by the universe
to figure itself out—and we
have only just begun.

NEIL DEGRASSE TYSON, ASTROPHYSICIST

21
SEPTEMBER

In times of stress, the best thing we can do for our children (and for each other) is to listen with our ears and our hearts and to be assured that our questions are just as important as our answers.

FRED ROGERS, FROM *MISTER ROGERS' NEIGHBORHOOD*

22
SEPTEMBER

That old September feeling, left over from school days, of summer passing, vacation nearly done, obligations gathering, books and football in the air. . . . Another fall, another turned page: there was something of jubilee in that annual autumnal beginning, as if last year's mistakes and failures had been wiped clean by summer.

WALLACE STEGNER, AUTHOR

23

SEPTEMBER

Even if I knew that
tomorrow the world
would go to pieces,
I would still plant
my apple tree.

———

MARTIN LUTHER, THEOLOGIAN

24

SEPTEMBER

Your life is an occasion. Rise to it.

MR. MAGORIUM'S WONDER EMPORIUM

25
SEPTEMBER

Dreams are only dreams until you wake up and make them real.

———

NED VIZZINI, AUTHOR

26
SEPTEMBER

You are the master
of your destiny. You
can influence, direct,
and control your own
environment. You can
make your life what
you want it to be.

NAPOLEON HILL, AUTHOR

Life, with its rules, its obligations, and its freedoms, is like a sonnet: You're given the form, but you have to write the sonnet yourself.

MADELEINE L'ENGLE, AUTHOR

28
SEPTEMBER

Whining is not only graceless, but can be dangerous. It can alert a brute that a victim is in the neighborhood.

MAYA ANGELOU, AUTHOR

29
SEPTEMBER

We must assume every event
has significance and contains
a message that somehow
pertains to our questions.
This especially applies to
what we used to call bad
things. . . . The challenge is to
find the silver lining in every
event, no matter how negative.

———

JAMES REDFIELD, AUTHOR

30
SEPTEMBER

In the sky there are always answers and explanations for everything: every pain, every suffering, joy and confusion.

ISHMAEL BEAH, AUTHOR

1
OCTOBER

DON'T JUDGE EACH DAY BY THE HARVEST YOU REAP BUT BY THE SEEDS THAT YOU PLANT.

ROBERT LOUIS STEVENSON, AUTHOR

2

OCTOBER

You're braver than you believe, stronger than you seem, and smarter than you think.

—

THE MANY ADVENTURES OF WINNIE THE POOH

3

OCTOBER

Pain, pleasure, and death are
no more than a process for
existence. The revolutionary
struggle in this process is a
doorway open to intelligence.

―――――

FRIDA KAHLO, ARTIST

4

OCTOBER

Inspiration is a guest that does not willingly visit the lazy.

PYOTR ILYICH TCHAIKOVSKY, COMPOSER

AT FIRST, DREAMS SEEM IMPOSSIBLE, THEN IMPROBABLE, AND EVENTUALLY INEVITABLE.

CHRISTOPHER REEVE, ACTOR

6

OCTOBER

When the whole world is silent, even one voice becomes powerful.

———

MALALA YOUSAFZAI, ACTIVIST

7

OCTOBER

If you care about what
you do and work hard at
it, there isn't anything you
can't do if you want to.

———

JIM HENSON, PUPPETEER

I must work harder to achieve my goal of not seeking approval from those whose approval I'm not even sure is important to me.

LAUREN GRAHAM, ACTOR

IF I DIE TOMORROW, NEXT YEAR OR WHENEVER IT MIGHT BE, I'LL KNOW I'VE HAD A GREAT LIFE.

MAGIC JOHNSON, ATHLETE

10
OCTOBER

Prejudice is a vagrant opinion without visible means of support.

AMBROSE BIERCE, JOURNALIST

11

OCTOBER

If you don't know what
you're willing to die for,
then you don't know
what you're living for.

———

NOAH WEINBERG, RABBI

12
OCTOBER

IT'S ENOUGH FOR ME TO BE SURE THAT YOU AND I EXIST AT THIS MOMENT.

GABRIEL GARCÍA MÁRQUEZ, AUTHOR

13

OCTOBER

You couldn't erase the past. You couldn't even change it. But sometimes life offered you the opportunity to put it right.

ANN BRASHARES, AUTHOR

14
OCTOBER

Sometimes you can learn, even from a bad experience. By coping you become stronger. The pain does not go away, but it becomes manageable.

———

SOMALY MAM, ADVOCATE

15

OCTOBER

If you want to be
proud of yourself,
then do things
in which you can
take pride.

KAREN HORNEY, PSYCHOANALYST

16

OCTOBER

Peace of mind comes when we exercise our right to be honest, especially with ourselves.

———

JACK R. ROSE, AUTHOR

When the creative impulse sweeps over you, grab it. . . . You grab it and honor it and use it, because momentum is a rare gift.

JUSTINA CHEN, AUTHOR

Rule your mind or it will rule you.

HORACE, POET

19

OCTOBER

Pay attention to what's happening around you. Read the book before you see the movie. Remember, though you, alone, are responsible for your own happiness, it's still okay to feel responsible for someone else's.

———

MICHAEL J. FOX, ACTOR

People often belittle
the place where
they were born
but heaven can be
found in the most
unlikely places.

MITCH ALBOM, AUTHOR

21
OCTOBER

*We are, all of us, exploring
a world none of us
understands . . . searching
for a more immediate,
ecstatic, and penetrating
mode of living . . . for the
integrity, the courage to
be whole, living in relation
to one another in the full
poetry of existence.*

———

HILLARY RODHAM CLINTON, U.S. SENATOR

22
OCTOBER

RECEIVE WITH SIMPLICITY EVERYTHING THAT HAPPENS TO YOU.

RASHI, BIBLE SCHOLAR

23
OCTOBER

Too many people out there tell us what we can and cannot do but . . . they don't know who we are, what's put in us.

ALEX ROGERS, AUTHOR

24

OCTOBER

Others may write from the head, but he writes from the heart, and the heart will always understand him.

WASHINGTON IRVING, AUTHOR

Happy is the man who has
broken the chains which hurt
the mind, and has given up
worrying once and for all. Be
patient and tough; one day this
pain will be useful to you.

———

OVID, POET

26
OCTOBER

Roam abroad in the world, and take thy fill of its enjoyments before the day shall come when thou must quit it for good.

SAADI, POET

We can
be friends.
We can be
anything we
want to be.

———

MURIEL BARBERY, AUTHOR

How quick and rushing life
can sometimes seem, when
at the same time it's so slow
and sweet and everlasting.

———

GRAHAM SWIFT, AUTHOR

29
OCTOBER

If you try to get rid of fear
and anger without knowing
their meaning, they will
grow stronger and return.

———

DEEPAK CHOPRA, AUTHOR

30
OCTOBER

WITHOUT INSPIRATION, WE'RE ALL LIKE A BOX OF MATCHES THAT WILL NEVER BE LIT.

DAVID ARCHULETA, VOCALIST

31
OCTOBER

Life, although it
may only be an
accumulation
of anguish, is
dear to me, and
I will defend it.

MARY SHELLEY, AUTHOR

Facing your fears robs them of their power.

MARK BURNETT, TELEVISION PRODUCER

2

NOVEMBER

Being a role model is the most powerful form of educating.

JOHN WOODEN, COACH

3
NOVEMBER

There are
darknesses in
life and there are
lights. You are one
of the lights.

BRAM STOKER, AUTHOR

4
NOVEMBER

The greenest of pastures are right here on earth.

JENNIFER DONNELLY, AUTHOR

5

NOVEMBER

To move, to breathe,
to fly, to float,
To gain all
while you give,
To roam the roads
of lands remote,
To travel is to live.

———

HANS CHRISTIAN ANDERSEN, AUTHOR

I've come to realize that sometimes, what you love most is what you have to fight the hardest to keep.

KIRSTEN HUBBARD, AUTHOR

7

NOVEMBER

Forbearance in the face of fate,
beauty constant under torture,
are not merely passive. They
are a positive achievement,
an explicit triumph.

———

THOMAS MANN, AUTHOR

8

NOVEMBER

Remember this, where there is life there is hope. You're alive. Embrace this, because you can do anything while there is breath in your body.

LOLA JAYE, AUTHOR

The greatest danger
for most of us lies not
in setting our aim
too high and falling
short; but in setting
our aim too low, and
achieving our mark.

MICHELANGELO, ARTIST

10

NOVEMBER

The joy that
you give to
others is the
joy that comes
back to you.

———

JOHN GREENLEAF WHITTIER, POET

11
NOVEMBER

On this Veterans Day, let us remember the service of our veterans, and let us renew our national promise to fulfill our sacred obligations to our veterans and their families who have sacrificed so much so that we can live free.

DAN LIPINSKI, CONGRESSMAN

12
NOVEMBER

I didn't know I had it in me.
There's more to all of us than
we realize. Life is so much
bigger, grander, higher, and
wider than we allow ourselves
to think. We're capable of so
much more than we allow
ourselves to believe.

———

QUEEN LATIFAH, PERFORMER

13

NOVEMBER

If I never got to make a living doing what I loved, I'd still do it—for fun and for free.

SUSAN E. ISAACS, AUTHOR

14
NOVEMBER

If pain is a pot of boiling water, humor can be the rising steam.

CAMERON CONAWAY, MMA FIGHTER

15

NOVEMBER

I am not afraid of tomorrow
for I have seen yesterday,
I have today and I know
Him who holds tomorrow
so I know tomorrow will
be beautiful for me.

JAACHYNMA N. E. AGU, AUTHOR

16
NOVEMBER

SEEK YOUR OWN ANSWERS IN LIFE, AND NOT WHAT OTHERS DICTATE TO YOU.

JEMINA AKHTAR, AUTHOR

17

NOVEMBER

I learned long ago that when change comes, you gotta slow down and take note of it. In the midst of that change is all the possibility in the world.

BERTICE BERRY, SOCIOLOGIST

18
NOVEMBER

We must reach out our hand
in friendship and dignity
both to those who would
befriend us and those who
would be our enemy.

ARTHUR ASHE, TENNIS PLAYER;
AND ARNOLD RAMPERSAD, AUTHOR

19

NOVEMBER

The reason most people give up so fast is that they look at how far they still have to go, instead of how far they have come.

———

ANONYMOUS

20
NOVEMBER

Motivation
gets you going;
inspiration
keeps you going.

———

TODD STOCKER, AUTHOR

21

NOVEMBER

WHAT WE CAN CHANGE IS OUR PERCEPTIONS, WHICH HAVE THE EFFECT OF CHANGING EVERYTHING.

DONNA QUESADA, AUTHOR

What is lovely
never dies,
but passes into
other loveliness,
Star-dust, or
sea-foam, flower,
or winged air.

———

THOMAS BAILEY ALDRICH, EDITOR

23
NOVEMBER

The stationary condition is the beginning of the end.

HENRI-FRÉDÉRIC AMIEL, PHILOSOPHER

24

NOVEMBER

To have more, you must genuinely thank more.

MADDY MALHOTRA, AUTHOR

A person is a person
because he recognizes
others as persons.

———

DESMOND TUTU, SOCIAL RIGHTS ACTIVIST
AND RETIRED ANGLICAN BISHOP

26

NOVEMBER

IMAGINATION IS THE TRUE MAGIC CARPET.

NORMAN VINCENT PEALE, AUTHOR

27

NOVEMBER

Doing what you wanted to do was the only training, and the only preliminary, needed for doing more of what you wanted to do.

KINGSLEY AMIS, AUTHOR

28

NOVEMBER

No one should ever despair because the entrance to his or her chosen career path is clogged. There is an ancient saying: "The persistent drip wears through stone."

———

KENTETSU TAKAMORI, AUTHOR

29

NOVEMBER

The heart of a person only beats when it's surrounded by blood, by family.

ERICA GOROS, AUTHOR

30
NOVEMBER

Most ideas are
born and lost
in isolation.

SCOTT BELSKY, AUTHOR

1

DECEMBER

*In recognizing the
humanity of our fellow
beings, we pay ourselves
the highest tribute.*

———

THURGOOD MARSHALL,
SUPREME COURT JUSTICE

2

DECEMBER

Inspiration comes unawares, from unaccountable sources that have nothing to do with planning or intelligence.

MAURICE CHEVALIER, ACTOR

3
DECEMBER

Real love is a
humble receptivity
of a silent heart
that is prepared to
melt and merge.

BANANI RAY AND AMIT RAY, AUTHORS

4

DECEMBER

YOUR BODY IS NOT A TEMPLE, IT'S AN AMUSEMENT PARK. ENJOY THE RIDE.

ANTHONY BOURDAIN, CHEF

5

DECEMBER

No matter how talented you are, if you don't persist the probability of achieving your goals is extremely small.

CAMILLA DORAND, AUTHOR

6
DECEMBER

If opportunity doesn't knock, build a door.

———

MILTON BERLE, ACTOR

7

DECEMBER

When you get older, you
know that life's mysteries
are revealed in the fullness
of time. All you have to do is
wait, watch, and be amazed.

———

LINDA GRAY, AUTHOR

8

DECEMBER

IT'S NEVER OVER TILL IT'S REALLY OVER IN YOUR MIND.

SANDHYA JANE, AUTHOR

9

DECEMBER

It can't be epic if there's no challenge to it.

JENNIFER E. SMITH, AUTHOR

10
DECEMBER

Today, people struggle to
find what's real. Everything
has become so synthetic
that a lot of people, all they
want is to grasp onto hope.

———

WYCLEF JEAN, MUSICIAN

Living is like tearing through
a museum. Not until later do
you really start absorbing
what you saw, thinking about
it, looking it up in a book, and
remembering—because you
can't take it all in at once.

AUDREY HEPBURN, ACTOR

12

DECEMBER

WELL-BEHAVED WOMEN SELDOM MAKE HISTORY.

LAUREL THATCHER ULRICH, HISTORIAN

13
DECEMBER

You can't stay in your corner of the Forest waiting for others to come to you. You have to go to them sometimes.

A. A. MILNE, AUTHOR

14

DECEMBER

There is neither happiness
nor misery in the world;
there is only the comparison
of one state with another,
nothing more.

———

ALEXANDRE DUMAS, AUTHOR

15

DECEMBER

Hope is the thing with feathers
That perches in the soul
And sings the tune
without the words
And never stops at all.

EMILY DICKINSON, POET

16

DECEMBER

I might have been given a bad break, but I've got an awful lot to live for.

LOU GEHRIG, ATHLETE

17
DECEMBER

LET US THINK ONLY OF THE GOOD DAYS THAT ARE TO COME.

———

AGATHA CHRISTIE, AUTHOR

18

DECEMBER

Once you have tasted flight, you will forever walk the earth with your eyes turned skyward, for there you have been, and there you will always long to return.

LEONARDO DA VINCI, POLYMATH

19

DECEMBER

Live in the present, remember the past, and fear not the future, for it doesn't exist and never shall. There is only now.

CHRISTOPHER PAOLINI, AUTHOR

20
DECEMBER

To see a World in a
Grain of Sand And a
Heaven in a Wild Flower,
Hold Infinity in the
palm of your hand
And Eternity in an hour.

———

WILLIAM BLAKE, POET

21

DECEMBER

Maybe everyone can
live beyond what
they're capable of.

MARKUS ZUSAK, AUTHOR

22

DECEMBER

*While no one can go back
and make a brand new
start, anyone can start now
and make a new ending.*

———

CHICO XAVIER, MEDIUM

23
DECEMBER

Happiness is only real when shared.

JON KRAKAUER, AUTHOR

That glimmer of light,
surrounded by so many
shadows, seemed to say
without words: Evil has not
yet taken complete dominion.
A spark of hope is still left.

———

ISAAC BASHEVIS SINGER, AUTHOR

25
DECEMBER

Our hearts grow tender with
childhood memories and
love of kindred, and we are
better throughout the year
for having, in spirit, become a
child again at Christmas-time.

LAURA INGALLS WILDER, AUTHOR

GREAT HEROES NEED GREAT SORROWS AND BURDENS, OR HALF THEIR GREATNESS GOES UNNOTICED.

PETER S. BEAGLE, AUTHOR

27

DECEMBER

The brick walls are there for a reason. The brick walls are not there to keep us out. The brick walls are there to give us a chance to show how badly we want something. Because the brick walls are there to stop the people who don't want it badly enough. They're there to stop the other people.

RANDY PAUSCH, COMPUTER SCIENTIST

*I've been fighting to be
who I am all my life.
What's the point of being
who I am, if I can't have
the person who was worth
all the fighting for?*

STEPHANIE LENNOX, AUTHOR

29

DECEMBER

A man who dares to waste one hour of time has not discovered the value of life.

CHARLES DARWIN, NATURALIST

30

DECEMBER

Have courage for the great
sorrows of life and patience
for the small ones; and
when you have laboriously
accomplished your daily
task, go to sleep in peace.

VICTOR HUGO, AUTHOR

31

DECEMBER

HOPE SMILES FROM THE THRESHOLD OF THE YEAR TO COME, WHISPERING "IT WILL BE HAPPIER . . ."

ALFRED LORD TENNYSON, POET

REFERENCES

Abel, L. Sydney. *Timothy Other: The Boy Who Climbed Marzipan Mountain*. Farmington, CO: Solstice, 2014.

Abercrombie, Joe. *Last Argument of Kings*. Amherst, NH: Pyr, 2008.

Abrahms, Irwin, ed. *Nobel Lectures, Peace 1971–1980*. Singapore: World Scientific Publishing, 1997.

Adams, Douglas. *The Long Dark Tea-Time of the Soul*. Portsmouth, NH: Heinemann, 1988.

Agu, Jaachynma N. E. *The Best Option*. Bloomington, IN: Xlibris, 2012.

Akhtar, Jemina. *Veil of Lies*. Jemina Akhtar, 2012.

Albom, Mitch. *The Five People You Meet in Heaven*. New York: Hyperion, 2003.

Alcorn, Randy C. *Money, Possessions, and Eternity*. Rev. and Updated. ed. Wheaton, IL: Tyndale House, 2003.

Aldrich, Thomas Bailey. "A Shadow of the Night, by Thomas Bailey Aldrich." PoetryArchive. Accessed October 18, 2015. www.poetry-archive.com/a /a_shadow_of_the_night.html.

Allende, Isabel. *The House of the Spirits*. Trans. Magda Bogin. New York: Everyman's Library, 2005.

Amiel, Henri-Frédéric. Goodreads. Accessed October 18, 2015. www.goodreads.com/quotes/201872-the-stationary-condition-is-the -beginning-of-the-end.

Amis, Kingsley. *Lucky Jim*. New York: Penguin, 1992.

Angelou, Maya. *Wouldn't Take Nothing for My Journey Now*. New York: Bantam, 1994.

Andersen, Hans Christian. *The Story of My Life*. New York: Hurd and Houghton, 1871.

REFERENCES

Antunes, Ana Claudia. *Pierrot & Columbine*. Ana Claudia Antunes, 2014.

Applegate, Katherine. "2015." *The One and Only Ivan*. Illus: Patricia Castelao. New York: HarperCollins, 2011.

Archuleta, David. *Chords of Strength: A Memoir of Soul, Song, and the Power of Perseverance*. New York: New American Library, 2010.

Arora, Manoj. *From the Rat Race to Financial Freedom: A Common Man's Journey*. Ahmedabad: Jaico Publishing House, 2013.

As Good as It Gets. Dir. James L. Brooks. Perf. Jack Nicholson, Helen Hunt, and Greg Kinnear. TriStar Pictures, 1997.

Ashby, Ruth, and Deborah Gore Ohrn, eds. *Herstory: Women Who Changed the World*. New York: Viking, 1995.

Ashe, Arthur, and Arnold Rampersad. *Days of Grace*. New York: Ballantine, 1994.

Aucoin, Kevyn. BrainyQuotes.com, accessed November 4, 2015. www.brainyquote.com/quotes/quotes/k/kevynaucoi358518.html.

Audubon, John James. "Explore 100 Famous Scientist Quotes Pages." Todayinsci. Accessed October 18, 2015. todayinsci.com/A/Audubon_John/AudubonJohn-Quotations.htm.

Augustine of Hippo. "The World Is a Book and Those Who Do Not Travel Read Only One Page." Lifehacker. Accessed October 18, 2015. lifehacker.com/5971748/the-world-is-a-book-and-those-who-do-not-travel-read-only-one-page.

Bach, Richard. *Illusions: The Adventures of a Reluctant Messiah*. New York: Bantam, 1989.

Baeli, Kelli Jae. *Immortality or Something Like it*. Eureka Springs, AR: Lesbian Literati Press, 2014.

Baldwin, James. "Sonny's Blues." *Going to Meet the Man*. New York: Dial, 1965.

Bambara, Toni Cade. AZquotes.com. Accessed November 5, 2015. www.azquotes.com/quote/546495.

Banda, Joyce. Swearing in Ceremony. April 7, 2012.

Barbery, Muriel. *The Elegance of the Hedgehog*. Trans. Alison Anderson. New York: Europa Editions, 2008.

Barker, Clive. *Imajica*. New York: HarperCollins, 1991.

Barr, Amelia E. *Remember the Alamo*. Whitefish, MT: Kessinger Publishing, 2004.

Barrie, J. M. *The Little White Bird*. London: Hodder and Stoughton, 1902.

Basil the Great. "No Need to Feel Like a Thief." NewsOK. Accessed October 18, 2015. newsok.com/article/1931552.

Beagle, Peter S. *The Last Unicorn*. New York: Viking, 1968.

Beah, Ishmael. *A Long Way Gone: Memoirs of a Boy Soldier*. New York: Farrar, Straus, and Giroux, 2007.

Beauvoir, Simone de. *La Vieillesse*. Paris: Gallimard, 1998.

Behn, Aphra. *The Lucky Chance*, 1686.

Bell, Alexander Graham. *The Seeds 4 Life*. Accessed October 18, 2015. www.theseeds4life.com/concentrate-all-your-thoughts-upon-the-work-at-hand -the-suns-rays-do-not-burn-until-brought-to-a-focus-alexander-graham-bell.

Belsky, Scott. *Making Ideas Happen: Overcoming the Obstacles Between Vision and Reality*. New York: Portfolio, 2012.

Berle, Milton. BrainyQuotes.com. Accessed November 4, 2015. www.brainyquote.com/quotes/topics/topic_inspirational.html#jtSi55kQ8ua0Ebcd.99.

Berry, Bertice. *Jim and Louella's Homemade Heart-Fix Remedy*. New York: Doubleday, 2002.

Berry, Wendell. *The Unsettling of America Culture & Agriculture*. Berkeley, CA: Counterpoint, 2015.

Bierce, Ambrose. Special Dictionary. Accessed October 18, 2015. www.special-dictionary.com/quotes/authors/a/ambrose_bierce/97065.htm.

Black, Ian Michael. Interviewed by Dan Schawbel. Forbes.com. Access November 4, 2015. www.forbes.com/sites/danschawbel/2012/04/12/michael-ian-black-on -his-career-expedia-and-social-media/.

Blake, William. "To See a World..." Poetry Lovers' Page. Accessed October 18, 2015. www.poetryloverspage.com/poets/blake/to_see_world.html.

Blume, Judy. *Summer Sisters: A Novel*. New York: Dell, 1999.

Bourdain, Anthony. *Kitchen Confidential.* New York: HarperCollins, 2007.

Boyle, T. C. Coraghessan. *The Tortilla Curtain.* New York: Viking, 1995.

Bradley, Marion Zimmer. *The Fall of Atlantis.* New York: Baen, 1987.

Brashares, Ann. *Girls in Pants: The Third Summer of the Sisterhood.* New York: Delacorte, 2006.

Brontë, Charlotte. *Jane Eyre.* Worldsworth Editions, 1997.

Brothers, Thomas, ed. *Louis Armstrong, in His Own Words: Selected Writings.* New York: Oxford University Press, 2001.

Brown, Andi. *Animal Cracker.* Seattle: CreateSpace Independent Publishing, 2013.

Brown, Brené. *Daring Greatly: How the Courage to Be Vulnerable Transforms the Way We Live, Love, Parent, and Lead.* New York: Avery, 2015.

Buddha, Gautama. "A Quote from Sayings of Buddha." Goodreads. Accessed October 18, 2015. www.goodreads.com/quotes/498520-no-one-saves-us -but-ourselves-no-one-can-and.

Buffalo Soldiers. Dir. Charles Haid. TNT. December 7, 1997.

Bukowski, Charles. *What Matters Most is How Well You Walk Through the Fire.* Black Sparrow Press, 1999.

Burnett, Mark. *Jump In!: Even If You Don't Know How to Swim.* New York: Ballantine, 2005.

Byrne, Jake. *First and Goal: What Football Taught Me About Never Giving Up.* Eugene, OR: Harvest House Publishers, 2015.

Camp, L. Sprague, and Fletcher Pratt. *Tales from Gavagan's Bar.* Expanded ed. Toronto: Bantam, 1980.

Capote, Truman. *Breakfast at Tiffany's: A Short Novel and Three Stories.* New York: Random House, 1958.

Carbone, Ute. *Blueberry Truth.* Warwick: Etopia, 2011.

Catherine the Great. "Stress Reduction | Mindfulness Muse." Mindfulness Muse. Accessed October 18, 2015. www.mindfulnessmuse.com/category /stress-reduction.

Cepeda, Raquel. *Bird of Paradise: How I Became Latina*. New York: Atria, 2013.

Chaucer, Geoffrey. *The Canterbury Tales*. Trans. David Wright. Oxford: Oxford University Press, 2011.

Chen, Justina. *North of Beautiful*. Boston: Little, Brown, 2009.

Chesterton, G. K. *Heretics*, 1905.

Chevalier, Maurice. *Bravo Maurice!: A Compilation From the Autobiographical Writings of Maurice Chevalier*. Australia: Allen & Unwin, 1973.

Child, Julia. *Julia's Kitchen Wisdom: Essential Techniques and Recipes from a Lifetime of Cooking*. New York: Knopf, 2009.

Chödrön, Pema. *When Things Fall Apart, Heart Advice for Difficult Times*. Berkeley, CA: Shambhala Publications, 2012.

Chopra, Deepak. *The Third Jesus: The Christ We Cannot Ignore*. New York: Three River, 2008.

Christie, Agatha. *Death Comes as the End*. New York: Dodd, Mead and Company, 1944.

Churchill, Winston. *My Early Life, 1874-1904*. New York: Scribner, 1996.

Clinton, Hillary Rodham. Commencement Address. Wellesley College, Wellesley, MA, June 1, 1969.

Coelho, Paulo. *Brida: A Novel*. Trans. Margaret Jull Costa. New York: Harper, 2008.

Colgan, Jenny. *Welcome to Rosie Hopkins' Sweetshop of Dreams*. London: Sphere, 2012.

Collins, Paul. *Drangonsight*. ReadHowYouWant, 2014.

Collins, Suzanne. *Catching Fire*. New York: Scholastic, 2009.

Conaway, Cameron. *Caged: Memoirs of a Cage-fighting Poet*. ThreeD, 2011.

Constantino, Rodrigo. *Prisoner of Freedom*. Soler, 2004.

Curie, Marie. Todayinsci. Accessed October 18, 2015. todayinsci.com/C /Curie_Marie/CurieMarie-Quotations.htm.

Dahl, Roald. *Charlie and the Great Glass Elevator*. Illus: Joseph Schindelman. New York: Knopf, 1972.

Dalai Lama. *The Dalai Lama's Book of Wisdom*. London: HarperCollins UK, 2000.

Darkholme, A. J. *Rise of the Morningstar*. Mistero Publishing, 2014.

Darwin, Charles. *The Life and Letters of Charles Darwin*. Ed. Francis Darwin. London: John Murray, 1887.

da Vinci, Leonardo. "The Da Vinci Codex: Treasured Sketches of Flight on Rare Display at Smithsonian." Washington Times. Accessed October 18, 2015. www.washingtontimes.com/news/2013/sep/12/the-da-vinci-codex-treasured -sketches-of-flight-on/?page=all.

deGrasse Tyson, Neil. "The Greatest Story Ever Told." *Natural History*, March 1, 1998.

DeLiso, Tony. *Legacy: The Power Within*. Writers Club, 2000.

Dessen, Sarah. *Just Listen*. New York: Speak, 2008.

DeSylva, Bud. *Look for the Silver Lining*. From the Movie, *Look for the Silver Lining*. T.B. Harms, 1920.

DeStefano, Lauren. *Wither*. New York: Simon & Schuster, 2011.

Diana, Princess of Wales. "Diana: The Legacy." The Huffington Post. Accessed October 18, 2015. www.huffingtonpost.com/david-allison/diana-the-legacy_b _1844945.html.

Dickens, Charles. *Our Mutual Friend*. Chapman & Hall, 1865.

Dickinson, Emily. "Hope Is the Thing with Feathers." Poets.org. Accessed October 18, 2015. https://www.poets.org/poetsorg/poem/hope-thing-feathers-254.

Donnelly, Jennifer. *Revolution*. New York: Ember, 2011.

Donoghue, Emma. *Room: A Novel*. Boston: Little, Brown/Back Bay, 2011.

Dorand, Camilla. *Back to Me: Changing How I Feel About My Mother, My Body, and Men*. Seattle: CreateSpace Independent Publishing, 2015.

Dostoyevsky, Fyodor. *The Idiot*. Ware, UK: Wordsworth Editions, 1996.

Douglass, Frederick. *Narrative of the Life of Frederick Douglass, An American Slave, Written by Himself, with Related Documents*. Ed. David W. Blight. 2nd ed. Boston: Bedford/St. Martin's, 2003.

Doyle, Arthur Conan. "A Scandal in Bohemia." *The Adventures of Sherlock Holmes*. George Newnes, 1891.

Dumas, Alexandre. *The Count of Monte Cristo*. Ware, UK: Wordsworth Editions, 1997.

Dylan, Bob. *Chronicles*. New York: Simon & Schuster, 2004.

Ebert, Roger. "Cinema: John Wayne as the Last Hero." *Time* magazine. August 8, 1969.

Eco, Umberto. *The Name of the Rose*. New York: Harcourt Brace Jovanovich, 1983.

Edison, Thomas. Mindbloom. Accessed October 18, 2015. tree.mindbloom.com/apps /inspiration/detail/image/07b94233-934b-465a-8148-e15c334edb4a/.

Edwards, Julie Andrews. *The Last of the Really Great Whangdoodles*. New York: Harper & Row, 1989.

Einstein, Albert. Philosiblog. Accessed October 18, 2015. philosiblog.com /2013/03/14/a-person-who-never-made-a-mistake-never-tried-anything-new/.

Elizabeth II, Queen. The Official Website of the British Monarchy. Accessed October 18, 2015. www.royal.gov.uk/imagesandbroadcasts /thequeenschristmasbroadcasts/christmasbroadcasts /christmasbroadcast1957.aspx.

Emerson, Ralph Waldo. "A Quote by Ralph Waldo Emerson." Goodreads. Accessed October 18, 2015. www.goodreads.com/quotes/548362-as-we-are-so-we-do -and-as-we-do.

Ende, Michael. *The Neverending Story*. Trans. Ralph Manheim. New York: Puffin, 1997.

Ephron, Nora. Commencement Address. Wellesley College, Wellesley, MA. June 3, 1996.

Epicurus. "Do Not Spoil What You Have By Desiring What You Have Not..." Gretchen Rubin. Accessed October 18, 2015. gretchenrubin.com/happiness_project/2009/12/do-not-spoil-what-you-have-by-desiring-what-you-have-not/.

Estés, Clarissa Pinkola. *The Faithful Gardener: A Wise Tale about That Which Can Never Die*. San Francisco: HarperOne, 1995.

Evanovich, Janet. *Seven up*. New York: St. Martin's, 2002.

Evans, Richard Paul. *The Gift*. New York: Simon & Schuster, 2007.

Fey, Tina. *Bossypants*. Boston: Little, Brown, 2011.

Fisher, M. F. K. *The Art of Eating*. 50th Anniversary ed. Hoboken, NJ: Wiley, 2004.

Fitzgerald, F. Scott. *The Great Gatsby*. London: Vintage Classic, 2011.

Flagg, Fannie. *I Still Dream about You: A Novel*. New York: Ballantine, 2010.

Flaubert, Gustave. Thrive. Accessed October 18, 2015. thrive.davidkanigan.com /post/83029896139/be-steady-and-well-ordered-in-your-life-so-that.

Fleming, Ian. *From Russia, with Love*. New York: Macmillan, 1957.

Fox, Michael J. *A Funny Thing Happened on the Way to the Future: Twists and Turns and Lessons Learned*. New York: Hyperion, 2010.

Francis of Assisi. Goodreads. Accessed October 18, 2015. www.goodreads.com /quotes/75455-he-who-works-with-his-hands-is-a-laborer-he.

Frank, Anne. *Anne Frank: Diary of a Young Girl*. West Hatfield, MA: Pennyroyal with Jewish Heritage Publishing, 1985.

Fulghum, Robert. *All I Really Need to Know I Learned in Kindergarten*. 15th Anniversary ed. New York: Ballantine, 2004.

Furman v. Georgia, 408 U.S. 238 (1972).

Gandhi, Mahatma. Totally Inspired Mind . . . Accessed October 18, 2015. totallyinspiredpc.wordpress.com/2013/11/26/each-night-when-i-go-to-sleep-i -die-and-the-next-morning-when-i-wake-up-i-am-reborn-gandhi/.

Gehrig, Lou. Lou Gehrig Appreciation Day. Yankee Stadium, New York, July 4, 1939.

Geisel, Theodor (Dr. Seuss). *On Beyond Zebra*. New York: Random House, 1955.

Gibran, Kahlil. *The Prophet*. New York: Knopf, 1923.

Gide, André. *Autumn Leaves*. Philosophical Library, 2007.

Gilbert, Elizabeth. *Eat, Pray, Love: One Woman's Search for Everything across Italy, India and Indonesia*. New York: Viking, 2006.

Gladwell, Malcolm. *Outliers: The Story of Success*. Boston: Little, Brown/Back Bay, 2011.

Glover, Robert A. *No More Mr. Nice Guy*. Philadelphia: Running, 2003.

Goethe, Johann Wolfgang von. Goodreads. Accessed October 18, 2015. www.goodreads.com/author/quotes/285217.Johann_Wolfgang_von_Goethe.

Goodreads. "A Quote from The Quran." Accessed October 18, 2015. www.goodreads.com/quotes/659080-don-t-tell-me-how-educated-you -are-tell-me-how.

Goros, Erica M. *The Daisy Chain*. Seattle: CreateSpace Independent Publishing, 2011.

Graham, Lauren. *Someday, Someday, Maybe: A Novel*. New York: Ballantine, 2014.

Gray, Linda. *The Road to Happiness Is Always under Construction*. Regan Arts, 2015.

Green, John. *An Abundance of Katherines*. New York: Dutton, 2006.

Guare, John. *Landscape of the Body*. New York: Dramatists Play Service, 1998.

Gutman, Bill. *Magic: More than a Legend: A Biography*. New York: Harper Paperbacks, 1992.

Hamilton, Alexander. *The Farmer Refuted*. 1774.

Hamilton-Ford, Jean. *Play.Create.Succeed*. Seattle: CreateSpace Independent Publishing, 2014.

Hannah, Kristin. *Firefly Lane: A Novel*. New York: St. Martin's Press, 2008.

Harris, Joanne. *Chocolat*. London: Doubleday, 1999.

Hawking, Stephen. *A Brief History of Time*. Updated and Expanded Tenth Anniversary ed. New York: Bantam, 1998.

Hazlitt, William. *Selected Essays of William Hazlitt, 1778-1830*. Ed. Geoffrey Keyens. London: Nonesuch, 1930.

Heaney, Seamus. *Beowulf: A New Verse Translation*. New York: W. W. Norton, 2001.

Heath, Chip, and Dan Heath. *Made to Stick: Why Some Ideas Survive and Others Die*. New York: Random House, 2007.

Henson, Jim, and The Muppets and Friends. *It's Not Easy Being Green: And Other Things to Consider*. New York: Hyperion, 2005.

Hesse, Hermann. *Siddhartha*. 1922.

Hill, Napoleon. *Think and Grow Rich*. Ralston Society, 1937.

Hillerman, Tony. *Coyote Waits*. New York: Harper, 2009.

Hitchens, Christopher. *Hitch-22: A Memoir*. New York: Twelve, 2010.

Hoffman, Alice. *Practical Magic*. New York: Berkley Group, 2003.

Hofstede, David. *Audrey Hepburn: A Bio-bibliography*. Westport, CT: Greenwood, 1994.

Homer. *Odyssey*. Trans. Stanley Lombardo. Indianapolis: Hackett, 2000.

Hooks, Bell, and Cornel West. *Breaking Bread: Insurgent Black Intellectual Life*. Boston: South End, 1991.

Horace. Goodreads. Accessed October 18, 2015. www.goodreads.com /quotes/980768-rule-your-mind-or-it-will-rule-you.

Horney, Karen. *Neurosis and Human Growth: The Struggle toward Self-realization*. New York: W. W. Norton, 1991.

Horst, Michelle. *Vaalbara Visions and Shadows*. Seattle: CreateSpace Independent Publishing, 2014.

Hubbard, Elbert. BrainyQuotes.com. Accessed November 4, 2015. www.brainyquote.com/quotes/authors/e/elbert_hubbard.html.

Hubbard, Kirsten. *Wanderlove*. Ember, 2013.

Hugo, Victor. Great Books Week. Accessed October 18, 2015. greatbooks.naiwe.com/tag/les-miserables.

Hurston, Zora Neale. *Their Eyes Were Watching God*. New York: Perennial Library, 1990.

Irving, Washington. *The Legend of Sleepy Hollow and Other Stories from the Sketch Book*. New York: Signet Classics, 2006.

Isaacs, Susan E. *Angry Conversations with God: A Snarky but Authentic Spiritual Memoir*. New York: Faith Words, 2011.

Isaacson, Walter. *Steve Jobs*. New York: Simon & Schuster, 2011.

Jacques, Brian. *The Taggerung: A Tale of Redwall*. Illus. Peter Standley. London: Hutchinson, 2001.

James, Henry. Personal Excellence. Accessed October 18, 2015. personalexcellence.co/quotes/2391.

Jane, Sandhya. *A Second Spring . . . Brings New Hope*. SJ-P, 2014.

Jaye, Lola. *By the Time You Read This*. New York: Avon, 2009.

Jean, Wyclef. "100 Greatest Artists, #11, Bob Marley." *Rolling Stone*, December, 2 2010.

Jefferson, Thomas. "Thomas Jefferson Quotes." RevWarTalk. Accessed October 18, 2015. www.revwartalk.com/Quotes-Thomas-Jefferson/when-angry-count-to-ten-before-you-speak-if-very-angry-count-to-one-hundred.html.

Johnson, George Clayton. "Nothing in the Dark." *The Twilight Zone*. CBS. January 5, 1962.

Johnson, Mat. *Loving Day: A Novel*. New York: Spiegel & Grau, 2015.

Johnson, Samuel. *The Rambler*. 1751.

Joyce, James. *Ulysses*. Paris: Sylvia Beach, 1922.

Kahlo, Frida. *The Diary of Frida Kahlo: An Intimate Self-Portrait*. New York: Abrams, 2005.

Kalidasa. "Look To This Day by Kalidasa." All Poetry. Accessed October 18, 2015. allpoetry.com/Look-To-This-Day.

Karr, Alphonse. *A Tour Round My Garden*. London: G. Routledge, 1855.

Kassem, Suzy. *Rise up and Salute the Sun: The Writings of Suzy Kassem*. Awakened, 2011.

Keller, Helen. "Keep Your Face to the Sun and You Will Never See the Shadows." Bubblews. Accessed October 18, 2015. www.bubblews.com/posts /keep-your-face-to-the-sun-and-you-will-never-see-the-shadows.

Keller, Timothy J. *Generous Justice: How God's Grace Makes Us Just*. New York: Riverhead, 2012.

Kenyon, Sherrilyn. *Invincible: The Chronicles of Nick*. New York: St. Martin's Griffin, 2011.

Kepnes, Caroline. *You: A Novel*. New York: Atria, 2015.

Kerouac, Jack. *The Dharma Bums*. New York: Penguin, 1990.

Kerry, John. Heavy. Accessed October 18, 2015. heavy.com/news/2015/09/9 -11-quotes-september-11th-remembering-sayings-george-bush-victims-from -firefighters/.

King, Martin Luther. *A Testament of Hope: The Essential Writings of Martin Luther King, Jr.* Ed. James Melvin Washington. San Francisco: Harper & Row, 1986.

King, Stephen. *On Writing: A Memoir of the Craft*. New York: Scribner, 2000.

Kingsolver, Barbara. *The Bean Trees: A Novel*. New York: Harper & Row, 1988.

Klam, Julie. *Friendkeeping: A Field Guide to the People You Love, Hate, and Can't Live without*. New York: Riverhead, 2012.

Koontz, Dean R. *Brother Odd*. New York: Bantam, 2006.

Kornfield, Jack. *Bringing Home the Dharma: Awakening Right Where You Are*. Berkeley, CA: Shambhala Publications, 2011

Krakauer, Jon. *Into the Wild*. New York: Villard, 1996.

Krause, Peter. Living Life Fully. Accessed October 18, 2015. www.livinglifefully.com /parents.htm.

Lane, Jennifer. *Streamline*. Dallas: Omnific Publishing, 2010.

Latifah, Queen. *Put on Your Crown: Life-Changing Moments on the Path to Queendom*. New York: Grand Central Publishing, 2010.

Lebowitz, Fran. *The Fran Lebowitz Reader*. New York: Vintage, 1994.

Le Carré, John. *Tinker, Tailor, Soldier, Spy*. New York: Knopf, 1974.

Leibovitz, Annie. *Annie Leibovitz at Work*. New York: Random House, 2008.

Lee, Harper. *To Kill a Mockingbird*. New York: HarperCollins, 1960.

Lee, Victor Robert. *Performance Anomalies*. Perimeter Six, 2012.

L'Engle, Madeleine. *A Wrinkle in Time*. New York: Farrar, Straus, and Giroux, 1962.

Lennox, Stephanie. *I Don't Remember You*. Seattle: CreateSpace Independent Publishing, 2010.

Levitt, Zola. *The Miracle of Passover*. Levitt, 1977.

Lichtenberg, Georg Christoph. "Social Justice & Civic Engagement." Hart House. Accessed October 18, 2015. harthouse.ca/learn-discover /social-justice-civic-engagement/.

Lincoln, Abraham. Letter to Isham Reavis. November 5, 1855.

Lipinski, Daniel. "Congressman Dan Lipinski: Floor Statements: In Honor of Veterans Day." Congressman Daniel Lipinski. Accessed October 18, 2015. www.lipinski.house.gov/floor-statements/in-honor-of-veterans-day/.

Lodder, Steve, and Stevie Wonder. *Stevie Wonder: A Musical Guide to the Classic Albums*. San Francisco: Backbeat, 2005.

Lombardi, Vince. BrainyQuotes.com, accessed November 4, 2015. www.brainyquote.com/quotes/quotes/v/vincelomba385070 .html#vOpX2ZFXfDOpuKWB.99.

London, Jack. Lifehack. Accessed October 18, 2015. www.lifehack.org/articles /featured/find-your-inspiration-jack-londons-way.html.

Lore, Pittacus. *The Power of Six*. New York: Harper, 2011.

Lubbock, John. *The Pleasures of Life*. London: Macmillan, 1887.

Luther, Martin. Beggars All: Reformation And Apologetics. Accessed October 18, 2015. beggarsallreformation.blogspot.com/2011/05/luther-plant-tree-at-end-of -world.html.

Malhotra, Maddy. *How to Build Self-Esteem and Be Confident Overcome Fears, Break Habits, Be Successful and Happy.* Seattle: CreateSpace Independent Publishing, 2013.

Mam, Somaly. *The Road of Lost Innocence: The True Story of a Cambodian Heroine.* New York: Spiegel & Grau, 2008.

Mandela, Nelson. *Long Walk to Freedom.* Randburg, South Africa: Macdonald Purnell, 1994.

Mankiller, Wilma, and Michael Wallis. *Mankiller: A Chief and Her People.* New York: St. Martin's Griffin, 2000.

Mann, Thomas. *Death in Venice.* S. Fischer Verlag, 1912.

Many Adventures of Winnie the Pooh, The. Dir. Wolfgang Reitherman & John Lounsbery. Perf. Sterling Holloway, John Fiedler, Paul Winchell. Walt Disney Productions, 1977.

Maraboli, Steve. *Unapologetically You: Reflections on Life and the Human Experience.* Port Washington, NY: Better Today, 2013.

Marcus Aurelius. Path Less Trodden. Accessed October 18, 2015. www.pathlesstrodden.com/2012/07/24/life-changing-quotes-never-let-the -future-disturb-you/.

Márquez, Gabriel García. One Hundred Years of Solitude. New York: Harper & Row, 1970.

Martel, Yann. *Life of Pi.* Toronto: Knopf Canada, 2001.

Marx, Groucho. "A Quote by Groucho Marx." Goodreads. Accessed October 18, 2015. www.goodreads.com/quotes/136001-if-you-re-not-having-fun-you -re-doing-something-wrong.

McCarthy, Cormac. *The Road.* New York: Vintage, 2006.

McCourt, Frank. *Angela's Ashes: A Memoir.* New York: Scribner, 1996.

McGill, Bryant, and Jenni Young. *Simple Reminders: Inspiration for Living Your Best Life.* SRN Publishing, 2015.

Michelangelo. ODesk. Accessed October 18, 2015. odesk.tumblr.com /post/92824933183/the-greatest-risk-to-man-is-not-that-he-aims-too.

Milne, A. A. *Winnie-the-Pooh*. London: Methuen & Co. Ltd., 1926.

Mitchell, David. *Cloud Atlas: A Novel*. New York: Random House, 2004.

Montgomery, Lucy Maud. *Anne of the Island*. L.C. Page & Co., 1915.

Moore, Christine Magnus. *Both Sides of the Bedside: From Oncology Nurse to Patient, an RN's Journey with Cancer*. Gray Matter Imprints, 2015.

Morrison, Toni. *Beloved*. New York: Knopf, 1987.

Morritt, Alex. *Impromptu Scribe*. Paxanax Press, 2014.

Morton, Kate. *The House at Riverton*. New York: Atria, 2008.

Mr. Magorium's Wonder Emporium. Dir. Zach Helm. Mandate Pictures, 2007.

Muir, John. *Our National Parks*. Boston: Houghton, Mifflin, 1901.

Murakami, Haruki. *What I Talk about When I Talk about Running*. London: Vintage, 2009.

Nelson, Willie. *It's a Long Story: My Life*. Boston: Little, Brown, 2015.

Nicholls, David. *One Day*. London: Hodder & Stoughton, 2009.

Ockler, Sarah. *Bittersweet*. New York: Simon Pulse, 2012.

Oliver, Lauren. *Hana*. New York: HarperCollins, 2012.

Oppel, Kenneth. *Skybreaker*. New York: Eos, 2006.

Ortner, Jessica. *The Tapping Solution for Weight Loss & Body Confidence: A Woman's Guide to Stressing Less, Weighing Less, and Loving More*. Hay House, 2014.

Ovid. PositiveSayings.net. Accessed October 18, 2015. positivesayings.net/happy-is-the-man-who-has-broken-the-chains-which-hurt-the-mind-and-has-given-up-worrying-once-and-for-all-be-patient-and-tough-one-day-this-pain-will-be-useful-to-you.

Paolini, Christopher. *Eldest*. New York: Alfred A. Knopf, 2005.

Parker, Elizabeth. *Paw Prints in the Sand*. Seattle: CreateSpace Independent Publishing, 2012.

Parks, Gordon. "Spurts of Enthusiasm and Lack of Interest." Success-Consciousness: *Mental Tools for a Great Life*. SuccessConsciousness.com. Accessed October 18, 2015. www.successconsciousness.com /spurts-enthusiasm.htm.

Pausch, Randy with Jeffrey Zaslow. *The Last Lecture*. New York: Hyperion, 2008.

Payne, Thomas. *Rights of Man*. London: J. S. Jordan, 1791.

Peale, Norman Vincent. *Three Complete Books: The Power of Positive Thinking; The Positive Principle Today; Enthusiasm Makes the Difference*. New York: Wings, 1992.

Pearce, Dan. *Single Dad Laughing: The Best of Year One*. Seattle: CreateSpace Independent Publishing, 2011.

Pessoa, Fernando. "Poems Inconjunctos." *Athena*. June 20, 1919.

Picasso, Pablo. *Pablo Picasso: Metamorphoses of the Human Form: Graphic Works, 1895–1972*. Ed. Roland Doschka. Munich: Prestel, 2000.

Poe, Edgar Allan. Edgar Allan Poe Society of Baltimore. Accessed October 18, 2015. www.eapoe.org/works/tales/mesmerd.htm.

Poehler, Amy. *Yes Please*. Dey Street, 2014.

Pope, Alexander. *An Essay on Criticism*. 1711.

Potter, Beatrix. "Old-Fashioned Charm: Happy Birthday to Beatrix Potter." Old-Fashioned Charm. Accessed October 18, 2015. old-fashionedcharm.blogspot. com/2011/07/happy-birthday-to-beatrix-potter.html.

Putnam, George Palmer. *Soaring Wings: A Biography of Amelia Earhart*. Harcourt, Brace and Company, New York, 1939.

Pratchett, Terry, and Stephen Baxter. *The Long War*. New York: Harper, 2013.

Quesada, Donna. *Buddha in the Classroom*. New York: Skyhorse Publishing, 2011.

Rashi. "A Serious Man,' At Sea In A Tragically Absurd World." NPR. Accessed October 18, 2015. www.npr.org/templates/story/story.php?storyId=113429323.

Ray, Amit. *World Peace: The Voice of a Mountain Bird*. Rishikesh: Inner Light, 2014.

Ray, Banani, and Amit Ray. *Awakening Inner Guru*. Inner Light Publishers, 2010.

Redfield, James. *The Celestine Prophecy*. New York: Warner, 1993.

Reeve, Christopher. *Nothing Is Impossible: Reflections on a New Life*. New York: Ballantine, 2004.

Renham, Lynda. *Coconuts and Wonderbras: A Romantic Comedy Adventure*. Combe: Raucous, 2012.

Rhimes, Shonda. Commencement Address. Dartmouth College Commencement. Dartmouth College, Hanover, NH, June 8, 2014.

Robbins, Anthony. *Get the Edge – A 7 Day Program to Transform Your Life*. Robbins Research, 2001.

Rogers, Alex. *I'm Only Human After All*. Alex Rogers, 2013.

Rogers, Fred. *The World According to Mister Rogers: Important Things to Remember*. New York: Hachette Books, 2003.

Roosevelt, Eleanor. *You Learn by Living: Eleven Keys for a More Fulfilling Life*. New York: Harper Perennial, 2011.

Roosevelt, Franklin D. "Remarks to the Daughters of the American Revolution." Washington, D.C. April 21, 1938. Lecture.

Roosevelt, Theodore. "9 Inspiring Quotes to Lift Your Spirits . . ." Allwomenstalk. Accessed October 18, 2015. lifestyle.allwomenstalk.com /inspiring-quotes-to-lift-your-spirits/2/.

Rose, Jack R. *The Cedar Post*. Heber City, UT: American Dream Makers, 2000.

Rostand, Edmond. *Cyrano De Bergerac: A Heroic Comedy in Five Acts*. Trans. Christopher Fry. Oxford: Oxford University Press, 1998.

Roth, Veronica. *Allegiant* New York: Katherine Tegen Books, 2013.

Rothfuss, Patrick. *The Wise Man's Fear*. New York: DAW, 2011.

Rowling, J. K. *Harry Potter and the Goblet of Fire*. London: Bloomsbury, 2000.

Ruth, Babe. Babe Ruth. Accessed October 18, 2015. www.baberuth.com/quotes/.

Saadi. Traveller Soul. Accessed October 18, 2015. travellersoul76.com /2014/01/03/52-of-the-most-inspiring-and-memorable-travel-quotes/.

Saint-Exupéry, Antoine de. *The Little Prince*. New York: Harcourt, Brace & World, 1943.

Sandberg, Sheryl. *Lean In: Women, Work, and the Will to Lead*. New York: Knopf, 2013.

Sanderson, Brandon. *The Rithmatist*. Illus. Ben McSweeney. New York: Tor Teen, 2013.

Saramago, Jose. *Blindness*. London: Harvill, 1997.

Scott, Elizabeth. *Perfect You*. New York: Simon Pulse, 2008.

Shakespeare, William. *Romeo and Juliet*. London: John Danter, 1597.

Sharma, Nihar. *Hijacked!* Nihar Sharma, 2014.

Shayne, Ann. *Bowling Avenue*. Nashville: Chenille, 2012.

Shelley, Mary Wollstonecraft. *Frankenstein; or, The Modern Prometheus*. London: Lackington, 1818.

Shelley, Percy Bysshe. "A Defence of Poetry." *Essays, Letters from Abroad, Translations and Fragments*. London: Edward Moxon, 1840.

Singer, Isaac Bashevis. *The Power of Light: Eight Stories for Hanukkah*. Illus: Irene Lieblich. New York: Farrar, Straus, and Giroux, 1990.

Sitting Bull. Sitting Bull: Famous Native American Indian Chief. Accessed October 18, 2015. www.warpaths2peacepipes.com/famous-native-americans /sitting-bull.htm.

Skloot, Rebecca. *The Immortal Life of Henrietta Lacks*. New York: Crown, 2010.

Smith, Barbara, ed. *Home Girls: A Black Feminist Anthology*. New Brunswick, NJ: Rutgers University Press, 2000.

Smith, Jennifer E. *Hello, Goodbye, and Everything in between*. Poppy, 2015.

Smith, Zadie. *White Teeth*. London: Hamish Hamilton, 2000.

Sobon, Nicole. *Program 13*. Seattle: CreateSpace Independent Publishing, 2012.

Soup, Cuthbert. *A Whole Nother Story*. New York: Bloomsbury, 2010.

Socrates. "The World's a Puzzle; No Need to Make Sense out of It." *Board of Wisdom*. BoardofWisdom.com. Accessed October 18, 2015. boardofwisdom.com/togo/Quotes/ShowQuote?msgid=589548#.ViP-U9KrSUk.

Spinelli, Jerry. *Stargirl*. New York: Scholastic, 2002.

Star Wars, Episode IV: A New Hope. Dir. George Lucas. Perf. Mark Hamill, Harrison Ford, Carrie Fisher, Peter Cushing and Alec Guinness. 20th Century Fox, 1977.

Stegner, Wallace. *Angle of Repose*. New York: Penguin, 1992.

Stein, Garth. *The Art of Racing in the Rain: A Novel*. New York: Harper, 2008.

Steinbeck, John. *Travels with Charley: In Search of America*. New York: Penguin, 1986.

Stephens, S. C. *Reckless*. Gallery, 2013.

Stern, Jessica. *Denial: A Memoir*. New York: Ecco, 2011.

Stern, Josh. *And That's Why I'm Single: What Good Is Having a Lucky Horseshoe up Your Butt When The Horse Is Still Attached?* BookBaby, 2009.

Stevenson, Robert Louis. Balanced Soul. Accessed October 18, 2015. ejimak.wordpress.com/2012/04/28/dont-judge-each-day-by-the-harvest-you-reap-but-by-the-seeds-you-plant-robert-louis-stevenson/.

Stocker, Todd. *Refined: Turning Pain into Purpose*. Seattle: CreateSpace Independent Publishing, 2012.

Stoker, Bram. *Dracula*. London: Archibald Constable and Company, 1897.

Stovel, DeeDee. *Picnic: 125 Recipes with 29 Seasonal Menus*. North Adams, ME: Storey, 2001.

Sugg, Chad. *Waking Up In Black and White*. lulu.com, February 2015.

Swift, Graham. *Tomorrow*. London: Picador, 2007.

Swindoll, Charles R. Thinkexist.com Charles R. Swindoll Quotes. Accessed November 4, 2015. http://thinkexist.com/quotes/charles_r._swindoll.

Tagore, Rabindranath. *Stray Birds*. New York: The Macmillan Company, 1916.

Takamori, Kentetsu. *Something You Forgot . . . along the Way: Stories of Wisdom and Learning.* Los Angeles: Ichimannendo Publishing, 2009.

Tallentyre, S. G. *The Friends of Voltaire.* London: Smith, Elder, & Co., 1906.

Tan, Amy. *The Hundred Secret Senses.* New York: G.P. Putnam's Sons, 1995.

Tchaikovsky, Pyotr Ilyich. CreatingMinds. Accessed October 18, 2015. creatingminds.org/quotes/inspiration.htm.

Tennyson, Alfred Lord. *The Foresters: Robin Hood and Maid Marian.* Kessinger Publishing, 2007.

Thoreau, Henry David. "Today's Quotes: Any Fool Can Make a Rule, and Any Fool Will Mind It." Daily Love with Mastin Kipp. Accessed October 18, 2015. thedailylove.com/todays-quotes-any-fool-can-make-a-rule-and-any-fool -will-mind-it/.

Tolkien, J. R. R. *The Fellowship of the Ring.* New South Wales, Australia: Allen & Unwin, 1954.

Tolstoy, Leo. *War and Peace.* Moscow: The Russian Messenger, 1869.

Torres, Dara, and Elizabeth Weil. *Age Is Just a Number: Achieve Your Dreams at Any Stage in Your Life.* New York: Broadway, 2010.

Tsukiyama, Gail. *The Street of a Thousand Blossoms.* New York: St. Martin's Griffin, 2008.

Tutu, Desmond. Address at His Enthronement as Anglican Archbishop of Cape Town. Cape Town, South Africa, September 7, 1986.

Tyson, Timothy B. *Blood Done Sign My Name.* New York: Crown, 2004.

Ulrich, Laurel Thatcher. *Well-behaved Women Seldom Make History.* New York: Vintage, 2008.

Vance, Ashlee. *Elon Musk: Tesla, SpaceX, and the Quest for a Fantastic Future.* New York: Ecco, 2015.

Van Gogh, Vincent, Arnold Pomerans, and Ronald de Leeuw. *The Letters of Vincent Van Gogh.* London: Penguin, 1997.

Verghese, A. *Cutting for Stone.* New York: Vintage, 2010.

Viorst, Judith. *Love & Guilt & the Meaning of Life, Etc.* New York: Simon & Schuster, 1979.

Virgil. *The Aeneid.* Trans. Robert Fitzgerald. Vintage Classics ed. New York: Vintage, 1990.

Vizzini, Ned. *It's Kind of a Funny Story.* New York: Miramax/Hyperion for Children, 2006.

Walker, Alice. *African American Quotes.* Accessed October 18, 2015. www.africanamericanquotes.org/life.html.

Warhol, Andy. *The Philosophy of Andy Warhol: From A to B and Back Again.* New York: Harcourt Brace Jovanovich, 1975.

Washington, George. Simple Thing Called Life. Accessed October 18, 2015. www.simplethingcalledlife.com/2014/george-washington-quotes/.

Waugh, Evelyn. *Brideshead Revisited; the Sacred and Profane Memories of Captain Charles Ryder.* Boston: Little, Brown, 1945.

Weinberg, Noah. AISH.com. Accessed November 4, 2015. www.aish.com/ci/s/My_Top_10_Quotes.html.

Whitman, Walt. The Cult of Genius. Accessed October 18, 2015. thecultofgenius.tumblr.com/post/6044675406/i-have-learned-that-to-be-with-those-i-like-is.

Whittier, John Greenleaf. DN Journal. Accessed October 18, 2015. www.dnjournal.com/archive/lowdown/2012/dailyposts/20121225.htm.

Wilde, Oscar. "Be Yourself, Everyone Else Is Already Taken: Transform Your Life With The Power of Authenticity." The Huffington Post. Accessed October 18, 2015. www.huffingtonpost.com/mike-robbins/be-yourself-everyone-else_b_185923.html.

Wilder, Laura Ingalls, and Rose Wilder Lane. *Little House Sampler.* Ed. William T. Anderson. New York: Perennial Library, 1989.

Winfrey, Oprah. *What I Know for Sure.* New York: Flatiron Books, 2014.

Wollstonecraft, Mary. *A Vindication of the Rights of Woman: With Strictures on Political and Moral Subjects.* Boston: Thomas and Andrews, 1792.

Wooden, Coach John. *Wooden.* New York: Contemporary, 1997.

Woolf, Virginia. *A Room of One's Own*. New York: Harcourt Brace & Co., 1989.

Yoshimoto, Banana. *Kitchen*. New York: Washington Square, 1993.

Young, Suzanne. *A Need So Beautiful*. New York: Balzer Bray, 2012.

Yousafzai, Malala. *I Am Malala: The Girl Who Stood up for Education and Was Shot by the Taliban*. Boston: Little, Brown, 2013.

Yu, Lu. "Philosophies for Life." Nourishing Buttons. Accessed October 18, 2015. nourishingbuttons.wordpress.com/2013/01/29/philosophies-for-life/.

Zusak, Markus. *I Am the Messenger*. New York: Alfred A. Knopf, 2006.

ABOUT THE
FOREWORD AUTHOR

MIKE ROBBINS is the author of three books, *Focus on the Good Stuff, Be Yourself: Everyone Else Is Already Taken*, and *Nothing Changes Until You Do*. He delivers keynotes and seminars around the world for clients such as Google, Gap, Microsoft, Schwab, eBay, and many others. He and his work have been featured in *O* Magazine, the *Wall Street Journal*, and the *Huffington Post*. His books have been translated into 12 different languages. For more about him and his work, visit www.mike-robbins.com.

9 781623 157166